APPLEWOOD'S
AMERICAN FRONTIER
SERIES

New English Canaan

Thomas Morton

APPLEWOOD BOOKS
Carlisle, Massachusetts

New English Canaan
was originally published in
1838

ISBN: 978-1-4290-4566-7

APPLEWOOD'S AMERICAN FRONTIER SERIES

Thank you for purchasing an Applewood book. Applewood reprints America's lively classics—books from the past that are still of interest to modern readers. This facsimile was printed using many new technologies together to bring our tradition-bound mission to you. Applewood's facsimile edition of this work may include library stamps, scribbles, and margin notes as they exist in the original book. These interesting historical artifacts celebrate the place the book was read or the person who read the book. In addition to these artifacts, the work may have additional errors that were either in the original, in the digital scans, or introduced as we prepared the book for printing. If you believe the work has such errors, please let us know by writing to us at the address below.

For a free copy of our current print catalog featuring our bestselling books, write to:

APPLEWOOD BOOKS
P.O. Box 27
Carlisle, MA 01741

For more complete listings, visit us on the web at:
www.awb.com

Prepared for publishing by HP

NEW ENGLISH CANAAN;

OR,

New Canaan,

CONTAINING

AN ABSTRACT OF *NEW ENGLAND.*

COMPOSED IN THREE BOOKES.

The first setting forth the Originall of the Natives, their Manners and Customs. Together with their tractable Nature and Love towards the English.

II. *The Natural Indowments of the Countrie, and what Staple Commodities it yeeldeth.*

III. *What People are planted there, their Prosperity, what remarkable Accidents have happened since the first planting of it; together with their Tenents and Practise of their Church.*

WRITTEN BY

THOMAS MORTON, of Cliffords Inn, Gent.

Upon ten Yeers Knowledge and Experiment of the Country.

Printed by *Charles Green.* 1632.

To the right honorable, the Lords and others of his Majesties most honorable privy Councell, Commissioners, for the Government of all his Majesties forraigne Provinces.

Right honorable,

THe zeale which I beare to the advancement of the glory of God, the honor of his Majesty, and the good of the weale publike, hath incouraged mee to compose this abstract, being the modell of a Rich hopefull and very beautifull Country, worthy the Title of Natures Masterpeece, and may be lost by too much sufferance. It is but a widowes mite, yet all that wrong and rapine hath left mee to bring from thence, where I have indeavoured my best, bound by my allegeance, to doe his Majesty service. This in all humility I present as an offering wherewith I prostrate my selfe at your honorable footstoole. If you please to vouchsafe, it may receave a blessing, from the Luster of your gracious Beames, you shall make your vassaile happy, in that hee yet doth live, to shew how ready hee is and alwayes hath bin, to sacrifice his dearest blood, as becometh a loyall subject, for the honor of his native Country. Being

your honors humble vassaile

THOMAS MORTON.

The Epistle to the Reader.

GENTLE READER,

I Present to the publike view an abstract of new England; which I have undertaken to compose by the incouragement of such genious spirits as have been studious of the inlargment of his Majesties Territories, being not formerly satisfied, by the relations of such as through haste, have taken but a superficiall survey thereof, which thing time hath enabled mee to performe more punctually to the life, and to give a more exact accompt of what hath been required; I have therefore beene willing to doe my indevoure to communicat the knowledge, which I have gained and collected together, by mine owne observation, in the time of my many yeares residence in those parts, to my loving Country men: For the better information of all such as are desirous to be made partakers of the blessings of God in that fertile Soyle, as well as those that, out of Curiosity onely have bin inquisitive after novelties. And the rather for that I have observed, how divers persons (not so well affected to the weale publike in mine opinion) out of respect to their owne private ends; have laboured to keepe both the practise of the people there, and the Reall worth of that eminent Country concealed from publike knowledge, both which I have abundantly in this discourse layd open, yet if it be well accepted, I shall esteeme my selfe sufficiently rewardded for my undertaking. and rest.

Your Wellwisher.

THOMAS MORTON.

In laudem Authoris.

T' Excuse the Author ere the worke be shewne
Is accusation in it selfe alone,
And to commend him might seeme oversight,
So divers are th' opinions of this age,
So quick and apt, to taxe the moderne stage,
That hard his taske, is that must please in all
Example have wee from great Cæsars fall,
But is the sonne to be dislik'd and blam'd,
Because the mole is of his face asham'd,
The fault is in the beast not in the sonne
Give sicke mouthes sweete meates fy they relish none,
But to the sound in censure he commends,
His love unto his Country his true ends,
To modell out a Land of so much worth,
As untill now noe traveller seth forth,
Faire Canaans second selfe, second to none,
Natures rich Magazine till now unknowne,
Then here survay, what nature hath in store,
And graunt him love for this, he craves no more.

R. O. Gen.

Sir Christoffer Gardiner, Knight.

In laudem Authoris.

THis worke a matchles mirror is that shewes,
The Humors of the seperatiste, and those
So truely personated by thy pen,
I was amaz'd to see't, herein all men,
May plainly see as in an inter-lude,
Each actor, figure and the scœne wel' view'd,
In Connick Tragick and in a pastorall stife,
For tyth of muit and Cummin shewes their life,
Nothing but opposition, gainst the right,
Of sacred Majestie men, full of spight,
Goodnes abuscing, turning vertue out
Of Dores, to whipping stocking and full bent,
To plotting mischeife, gainst the innocent,
Burning their houses, as if ordained by fate,
In spight of Lawe, to be made ruinate,
This taske is well perform'd and patience be,
Thy present comfort and thy constancy,
Thine honor, and this glasse where it shall come,
Shall sing thy praises till the day of doome.

Sir. G. C.

In laudem Authoris.

BVt that I rather pitty I confesse,
The practise of their Church, I could expresse
Myselfe a Satyrist; whose smarting fanges,
Should strike it with a palsy, and the panges,
Beget a feare, to tempt the Majesty,
Of those, or mortall Gods, will they defie
The Thundering Jove, like children they desire,
Such is their zeale, to sport themselves with fire,
So have I seene an angry Fly, presume,
To strike a burning taper, and consume
His feeble wings, why in an aire so milde,
Are they so monstrous growne up, and so vilde,
That Salvages can of themselves espy
Their errors, brand their names with infamy,
What is their zeale for blood, like Cyrus thirst,
Will they be over head and eares, a curst
A cruell way to found a Church on, noe,
T'is not their zeale, but fury blinds them soe
And pricks their malice on like fier to joyne,
And offer up the sacrifice of Kain;
Jonas, thou hast done well, to call those men
Home to repentance, with thy painefull pen.

F. C. Armiger.

NEW ENGLISH CANAAN,

OR

NEW CANAAN.

The Authors Prologue.

IF art & industry should doe as much
As Nature hath for Canaan, not such
Another place, for benefit and rest,
In all the universe can be possest,
The more we proove it by discovery,
The more delight each object to the eye
Procures, as if the elements had here
Bin reconcil'd, and pleas'd it should appeare,
Like a faire virgin, longing to be sped,
And meete her lover in a Nuptiall bed,
Deck'd in rich ornaments t' advaunce her state
And excellence, being most fortunate,
When most enjoy'd, so would our Canaan be
If well employ'd by art and industry
Whose offspring, now shewes that her fruitfull wombe
Not being enjoy'd, is like a glorious tombe,
Admired things producing which there dye,
And ly fast bound in darck obscurity,
The worth of which in each particuler,
Who list to know, this abstract will declare.

NEW ENGLISH CANAAN, OR NEW CANAAN.

The first Booke.

Containing the originall of the Natives, their manners, & Customes, with their tractable nature and love towards the English.

Chap. I.

Prooving New England the principall part of all America, and most commodious and fitt for habitation.

THe wise Creator of the universall Globe, hath placed a golden meane betwixt two extreames: I meane the temperate Zones, betwixt the hote and cold; and every Creature, that participates of Heavens blessings, with in the Compasse of that golden meane, is made most apt and fit, for man to use, who likewise by that wisedome is ordained to be the Lord of all. This globe may be his glasse, to teach him how to use moderation, and discretion, both in his actions and intentions. The wise man sayes, give mee neither riches nor poverty; why? Riches might make him proud like Nebuchadnezar, and poverty despaire,

Vse of vegetatives. like Iobs wife, but a meane betweene both. So it is likewise in the use of Vegetatives, that which hath too much Heate or too much Colde, is said to be venenum, so in the use of sensitives, all those Animals, of what genus or species soever they be, if they participate of heate or cold, in the superlative, are said to be *Inimica naturæ*, as in some Fishes about the Isle of Sall, and those Ilandes adjoyninge, betweene the Tropickes, their participatinge of heate and cold, in the superlative is made most manifest, one of which, poysoned a whole Ships company that eate of it. And so it is in Vipers, Toades, and Snakes, that have heate or cold in the superlative degree.

Fish poysonous about the Isle of Sall.

Therefore the Creatures that participate of heate and cold in a meane, are best and holsomest: And so it is in the choyse of love, the middell Zone betweene the two extreames is best, and it is therefore called *Zona temperata*, and is in the golden meane; and all those Lands lying under that Zone, most requisite and fitt for habitation. In Cosmography, the two extreames are called, the one *Torrida Zona*, lying betweene the Tropickes, the other *Frigida Zona*, lying neare the Poles: all the landes lying under, either of these Zones, by reason, they doe participate too much of heate or cold, are very inconvenient, and are accompanied with many evils. And allthough I am not of opinion with Aristotle, that the landes under *Torrida Zona*, are alltogether uninhabited, I my selfe having beene so neare the equinoctiall line, that I have had the Sunn for my Zenith, and seene proofe to the contrary, yet cannot I deny, but that it is accompanied with many inconveniences, as that Fish and Flesh both will taint in those partes, notwithstanding the use of Salt which cannot be wanting there, ordained by natures hande-worke. And that is a great hinderance to the settinge forth and supply of navigation, the very Sinewes of a flourishing Commonwealth. Then barrennesse, caused through want of raines, for in most of those partes of the world it is seldome accustomed to raine, untill the time of the Tornathees (as the Portingals phrase is, who lived there) and then it will raine about 40. dayes together, which moisture serveth to fructify the earth for all the yeare after duringe which time is seene no raine at all: the heate and cold, and length of day and night, being much alike, with little difference. And these raines are caused by the turning of the windes, which else betweene the Tropickes, doe blow Trade, that is allwayes one way. For next the Tropicke of Cancer it is constantly North-East, and next the Tropicke of

Zona temperata, the Golden meane.

Salt aboundeth under the Tropicks.

Raine 40. dayes about August betweene Cancer and the Line.

Capricorne it is Southwest; so that the windes comming from the Poles, do keepe the aire in those partes coole, and make it temperate and the partes habitable, were it not for those and other inconveniences.

This *Torrida Zona* is good for Grashoppers: and *Zona Temperata* for the Ant and Bee. But *Frigida Zona* good for neither, as by lamentable experience of Captaine Davis Fate, is manifest, who in his inquest of the Northwest passage for the East India trade was frozen to death. And therefore for *Frigida Zona*, I agree with Aristotle, that it is unfit for habitation: and I know by the Course of the cælestiall globe, that in Groeneland many Degrees short of the Pole Articke, the place is too cold, by reason of the Sunns absence almost six monthes, and the land under the continuall power of the frost; which thinge many more Navigators have prooved with pittifull experience of their wintringe there, as appeareth by the history, I thinke, they will not venture to winter there againe for an India mine.

Capt. Davis froze to death.

Groene Land too cold for habitation.

And as it is found by our Nation under the Pole Articke, so it is likewise to be found under the Antarticke Pole, yet what hazard will not an industrious minde, and couragious spirit undergoe, according to that of the Poet. *Impiger extremos currit Mercator ad Indos per mare pauperiem fugiens, per saxa, per ignes.* And all to gett and hord up like the Ant and the Bee, and yet as Salomon saith, he cannot tell whether a foole or a wise man shall enjoy it. Therefore let us leave these two extreames, with their inconveniences, and indeavour to finde out this golden meane, so free from any one of them. Behold the secret wisedome of Allmighty God, and love unto, our Salomon to raise a man of a lardge hart, full of worthy abilities to be the Index or Loadstarre, that doth point out unto the English Nation, with ease and comfort how to finde it out. And this the noble minded Gentleman, Sir Ferdinando Gorges Knight, zealous for the glory of God, the honor of his Majesty, and the benefit of the weale publicke, hath done a great worke for the good of his Country.

Sir Ferdinando Gorges the originall cause of plantinge New England.

And herein this, the wondrous wisedome and love of God, is shewne, by sending to the place his Minister, to sweepe away by heapes the Salvages, and also giving him length of dayes, to see the same performed after his enterprise was begunne, for the propagation of the Church of Christ.

The Salvages dyed of the plague

This judicious Gentleman, hath found this golden meane, to be scituated about the middle of those two extreames, and for directions you may proove it thus: Counting the space betweene the Line and either of the Poles, in true proportion, you shall finde it to be 90. Degrees: then must we finde the meane, to be neare unto the Center of 90. and that is about 45. Degrees, and then incline unto the Sotherne side of that Center, properly for the benefit of heate, remembringe that *Sol & Homo generàt hominem;* and then keepe us on that same side, and see what Land is to be found there, and we shall easily discerne that new England is on the South side of that Center.

New England is placed in the golden meane.

For that Country doth beginne her boundes at 40. Degrees of Northerne latitude, and ends at 45. Degrees of the same latitude, and doth participate of heate and cold indifferently, but is oppressed with neither: and therefore may be truly sayd to be within the compasse of that golden meane, most apt and fit for habitation and generation, being placed by Allmighty God the great Creator, under that Zone, called *Zona temperata*, and is therefore most fitt for the generation and habitation of our English nation, of all other, who are more neere neighbours to the Northerne Pole, whose Land lyeth betweene 50. and 54 Degrees of the selfesame latitude: now this new England though it be nearer to the line, then that old England by 10. Degrees of latitude, yet doth not this exceede that other in heate or cold, by reason of the cituation of it; for as the Coast lyeth, being circularly Northeast and Southwest, opposite towards the Sunnes risinge, which makes his course over the Ocean, it can have litle or no reflecting, heat of the Sunbeames, by reason of the continuall motion of the waters, makinge the aire there the cooler and the constanter; so that for the temperature of the Climent, sweetnesse of the aire, fertility of the Soile, and small number of the Salvages (which might seeme a rubb in the way of an effeminate minde,) this Country of new England is by all judicious men, accounted the principall part of all America, for habitation and the commodiousnesse of the Sea, Ships there not being subject to wormes, as in Virginea and other places, and not to be paraleld in all Christendome. The Massachussets being the middell part thereof, is a very beautifull Land not mountany, nor inclininge to mountany, lyeth in 42. Degrees, and 30. minutes, and has as yet the greatest number of inhabitants, and hath a very large bay to it, divided by Islands into 4 great bayes, where shippinge may safely ride all windes and weathers in those partes being not so violent as in England by many Degrees, for there

New England 10. Degrees neerer the line then old England.

The Massachussets in the middel of New England.

The Windes not so violent in New England.

are no shrubbs seene, to leane from the windes as by the Sea Coast of England, I have seene them leane, and the groundage is a sandy sleech free from rocks to gaule Cables, but is good for anchorage, the rest of the Planters are disperst among the Coasts betweene 41. and 44. Degrees of Latitude, and as yet, have very little way into the iland, the riches of which Country I have set forth in this abstract as in a Landskipp, for the better information of the Travellers, which hee may peruse and plainely perceave by the demonstration of it, that it is nothing inferior to Canaan of Israel, but a kind of paralell to it, in all points.

Chap. II.

Of the originall of the Natives.

IN the yeare since the incarnation of Christ, 1622. it was my chance to be landed in the parts of New England, where I found two sortes of people, the one Christians, the other Infidels, these I found most full of humanity, and more friendly then the other: as shall hereafter be made apparant in Dew-Course, by their severall actions from time to time, whilest I lived among them After my arrivall in those partes, I endeavoured by all the wayes and meanes that I could to find out from what people or nation, the Natives of New England might be conjectured originally to proceede, & by continuance & conversation amongst them, I attaned to so much of their language, as by all probable conjecture may make the same manifest, for it hath been found by divers, and those of good judgement that the Natives of this Country, doe use very many wordes both of Greeke and Latine, to the same signification that the Latins and Greekes have done, as *en animia*, when an Indian expresseth, that hee doth any thing with a good will; and *Pascopan* signifieth gredy gut, this being the name of an Indian that was so called of a Child, through the greedinesse of his minde, and much eating, for *Pasco* in Latine signifieth to feede, and *Pan* in Greeke signifieth all, and *Pasco nantum, quasi pasco nondum*, halfe starved, or not eating, as yet; *Equa coge*, set it upright, *Mona* is an Island in their language, *quasi Monon*, that is alone, for an Island is a peece or plott of ground standing alone, and devided from the mane Land by force of water.

The Natives have a mixed language.

Pasco Pan greedy gutt.

Mona an Island.

Cos a Whetstone. *Cos* is a Whetstone with them. *Hame* an instrument to take Fish, many places doe retaine the name of *Pan*, as Pantneket and *Matta pan*, so that it may be thought that these people heretofore, have had the name of *Pan the Shepheards God.* *Pan* in great reverence and estimation, and it may bee have worshipped *Pan* the great God of the Heathens: Howsoever they doe use no manner of worship at all now: and it is most likely that the Natives of this Country, are descended from people bred upon that part of the world, which is towardes the Tropicke of Cancer, for they doe still retaine the memory of some of the Starres one that part of thea Cælestiall Globe, as the North-starre, which with them is called Maske, for Maske in their Language signifieth a Beare, and they doe divide the windes into eight partes, and it seemes originally, have had some literature amongst them, which time hath Cancelled and worne out of use, and where as it hath beene the opinion of some men, which shall be nameles, that the Natives of New-England may proceede from the race of the Tartars, and come from Tartaria into those partes, over the frozen Sea.

Not to proceede from the Tartars. I see no probality for any suoh Conjecture, for as much, as a people once setled, must be remooved by compulsion, or else tempted thereunto in hope of better fortunes, upon commendations of the place, unto which they should be drawne to remoove, and if it may be thought, that these people came over the frozen Sea, then would it be by compulsion, if so, then by whome, or when? or what part of this *No part of America knowne to be neare Tartary.* mane continent may be thought to border upon the Country of the Tartars, it is yet unknowne, and it is not like, that a people well enough at ease, will of their one accord undertake to travayle over a Sea of Ice, considering how many difficulties they shall encounter with, as first whether there be any Land at the end of their unknowne way, no Land beinge in view, then want of Food to sustane life in the meane time upon that Sea of Ice, or how should they doe for Fuell, to keepe them at night from freezing to death, which will not bee had in such a place, but it may perhaps be granted that the Natives of this Country might originally come of the scattered Trojans: For after that Brutus, who was the forth from Aneas, left Latium upon the conflict *Why Brutus left Latium.* had with the Latines, (where although hee gave them a great overthrow, to the Slaughter of their grand Captaine and many other of the Heroes of Latium, yet hee held it more safety to depart unto some other place, and people, then by staying to runne the hazard of an unquiet life or doubtfull Conquest, which as history maketh mention hee performed ;) this people were dispersed there is no question, but the people that lived with him, by reason of their conversation with the Græcians and Latines, had a mixed language that participated of both, whatsoever was that which was proper to their owne nation at first ; I know not for this is commonly seene where 2. nations traffique together, the one indevouring to understand the others meaning makes thē both many times speak a mixed language, as is approoved by the Natives of New England, through the coveteous desire they have, to commerce with our nation, and wee with them.

Two nations meetinge make a mixed language.

And when Brutus did depart from Latium, we doe not finde that his whole number went with him at once, or arrived at one place ; and being put to Sea might encounter with a storme, that would carry them out of sight of Land, and then they might sayle God knoweth whether, and so might be put upon this Coast, as well as any other ; Compasse I beleeve they had none in those dayes ; Sayles they might have (which Dædalus the first inventor thereof) left to after ages, having taught his Sonne Icarus the use of it, who to his Cost found how dangerous it is, for a Sonne not to observe the precepts of a wise Father, so that the Icarian Sea, now retaines the memory of it to this day, and Victuals they might have good store, and many other things fittinge, oares without all question, they would store themselves with, in such a case, but for the use of Compasse there is no mention made of it at that time (which was much about Sauls time the first that was made King of Israell.) Yet it is thought (and that not without good reason for it) the use of the Loadstone, and Compasse was knowne in Salomons time, for as much as hee sent Shippes to fetch of the gould of Ophir, to adorne and bewtify that magnificent Temple of Hierusalem, by him built for the glory of Almighty God, and by his speciall appointment : and it is held by Cosmographers to be 3. yeares voyage from Hierusalem to Ophir, and it is conceaved that such a voyage could not have beene performed, without the helpe of the Loadstone and Compasse.

Dædalus the first that used Sayles.

Icarus the second that used Sayles.

Troy destroyed about Sauls time.

The Loadstone in Salomons time.

And why should any man thinke, the Natives of New England, to be the gleanings of all Nations, onely because by the pronunciation and termination their words seeme to trench upon severall languages, when time hath not furnished him with the interpretation thereof, the thinge that must induce a man of reasonable capacity to any manner of conjecture, of their originall, must by the sence and signification of the words, principally to frame this argument by, when hee shall drawe to any conclusion thereupon, otherwise hee shall but runne rounde about a maze (as some of the fantasticall tribe use to do about the tythe of muit and comin.) Therefore since I have had the approbation of Sir Christopher gardiner Knight an able gentl. that lived amongst them & of David Tompson a Scottish gentl. that likewise was conversant with those people both Scollers and Travellers that were diligent in taking notice of these things as men of good judgement. And that have bin in those parts any time; besides others of lesse, now I am bold to conclude that the originall of the Natives of New England may be well conjectured to be from the scattered Trojans, after such time as Brutus departed from Latium.

Chap. III.

Of a great mortality that happened amongst the Natives of New England neere about the time, that the English came there to plant.

IT fortuned some few yeares, before the English came to inhabit at new Plimmouth in New England; that upon some distast given in the Massachusetts bay, by Frenchmen, then trading there with the Natives for beaver, they set upon the men, at such advantage, that they killed manie of them burned their shipp then riding at Anchor by an Island there, now called Peddocks Island in memory of Leonard Peddock that landed there (where many wilde Anckies haunted that time which hee thought had bin tame, distributing them unto 5. Sachems which were Lords of the severall territories adjoyninge, they did keepe them so longe as they lived, onely to sport themselves at them, and made these five Frenchmen fetch them wood and water, which is the generall worke that they require of a servant, one of these five men out livinge the rest had learned so much of their language, as to rebuke them for their bloudy deede, saying that God would be angry with them for it; and that hee would in his displeasure destroy them; but the Salvages (it seemes boasting of their strenght,) replyed and sayd, that they were so many, that God could not kill them.

Five Frenchmen kept by the Salvages.

The Plague fell on the Indians.

But contrary wise in short time after, the hand of God fell heavily upon them, with such a mortall stroake, that they died on heapes, as they lay in their houses and the living; that were able to shift for themselves would runne away, & let them dy, and let there Carkases ly above the ground without buriall. For in a place where many inhabited, there hath been but one left a live, to tell what became of the rest, the livinge being (as it seemes) not able to bury the dead, they were left for Crowes, Kites, and vermin to pray upon. And the bones and skulls upon the severall places of their habitations, made such a spectacle after my comming into those partes, that as I travailed in that Forrest, nere the Massachussets, it seemed to mee a new found Golgatha.

The livinge not able to bury the dead.

But otherwise it is the custome of those Indian people, to bury their dead ceremoniously, and carefully, and then to abandon that place, because they have no desire the place should put them in minde of mortality: and this mortality was not ended, when the Brownists of new Plimmouth were setled at Patuxet in New England, and by all likelyhood the sicknesse that these Indians died of, was the Plague, as by conference with them since my arrivall, and habitation in those partes, I have learned. And by this meanes there is as yet but a small number of Salvages in New England to that, which hath beene in former time, and the place is made so much the more fitt, for the English Nation to inhabit in, and erect in it Temples to the Glory of God.

2. Sam. 24.

Chap. IV.

Of their Houses and Habitations.

THe Natives of New England are accustomed to build them houses, much like the wild Irish, they gather Poles in the woodes and put the great end of them in the ground, placinge them in forme of a circle or circumference, and bendinge the topps of them in forme of an Arch, they bind them together with the Barke of Walnut trees, which is wondrous tuffe, so that they make the same round on the Topp.

For the smooke of their fire, to assend and passe through? these they cover with matts, some made of reeds, and some longe flagges, or sedge finely sowed together with needles made of the splinter bones of a Cranes legge, with threeds, made of their Indian hempe, which their groueth naturally, leaving severall places for dores, which are covered with mats, which may be rowled up, and let downe againe at their pleasures, making use, of the severall dores, according as the winde sitts, the fire is alwayes made in the middest of the house, with winde fals commonly: yet some times they fell a tree, that groweth neere the house and by drawing in the end thereof maintaine the fire on both sids, burning the tree by Degrees shorter and shorter, untill it be all consumed; for it burneth night and day, their lodging is made in three places of the house about the fire they lye upon plankes commonly about a foote or 18. inches above the ground raised upon railes that are borne up upon forks they lay mats under them, and Coates of Deares skinnes otters beavers Racownes and of Beares hides, all which they have dressed and converted into good lether with the haire on for their coverings and in this manner they lye as warme as they desire in the night they take their rest, in the day time, either the kettle is on with fish or flesh, by no allowance: or else, the fire is imployed in roasting of fishes, which they delight in, the aire doeth beget good stomacks, and they feede continually, and are no niggards of their vittels, for they are willing, that any one shall eate with them, Nay if any one, that shall come into their houses, and there fall a sleepe, when they see him disposed to lye downe, they will spreade a matt for him, of their owne accord, and lay a roule of skinnes for a boulster, and let him lye? if hee sleepe untill their meate be dished up, they will set a wooden boule of meate by him that sleepeth, & wake him saying Cart up keene Meckin: That is, if you be hungry, there is meat for you, where if you will eate you may, such is their Humanity.

Likewise when they are minded to remoove, they carry away the mats with them, other materiales the place adjoyning will yeald, they use not to winter and summer in one place, for that would be a reason to make fuell scarse, but after the manner of the gentry of Civilized natives, remoove for their pleasures, some times to their hunting places where they remaine keeping good hospitality, for that season; and sometimes to their fishing places, where they abide for that season likewise: and at the spring, when fish comes in plentifully, they have meetinges from severall places, where they exercise themselves in gaminge, and playing of juglinge trickes, and all manner of Revelles, which they are delighted in, that it is admirable to behould, what pastime they use, of severall kindes, every one striving to surpasse each other, after this manner they spend their time.

Chap. V.

Of their Religion.

IT has bin a common receaved opinion from Cicero, that there is no people so barbarous, but have some worshipp, or other in this particular, I am not of opinion therein with Tully; and surely, If hee had bin amongst those people so longe as I have bin, and conversed so much with them, touching this matter of Religion, hee would have changed his opinion, neither should we have found this error, amongst the rest, by the helpe of that wodden prospect, if it had not been so unadvisedly built upon such highe land as that Coast, (all mens judgements in generall,) doth not yeeld, had hee but taken the judiciall councell of Sir William Alexander, that setts this thing forth in an exact and conclusive sentence; if hee be not too obstinate? hee would graunt that worthy writer, that these people are *sine fide, sine lege, & sine rege,* and hee hath exemplified this thinge by a familiar demonstration, which I have by longe experience observed to be true.

And me thinks, it is absurd to say they have a kinde of worship, and not able to demonstrate whome or what it is they are accustomed to worship. For my part I am more willing to beleeve that the Elephants (which are reported to be the most intelligible of all beasts) doe worship the moone, for the reasons given by the author of this report as Mr. Thomas May, the minion of the Muses dos recite it in his contimation, of Lucas historicall poem, rather then this man, to that I must bee constrained, to conclude against him, and Cicero; that the Natives of New England have no worship nor religion at all, and I am sure it has been so observed by those that neede not the helpe of a wodden prospect for the matter.

Chap. VI.

Of the Indians apparrell.

THe Indians in these partes do make their apparrell, of the skinnes of severall sortes of beastes, and commonly of those, that doe frequent those partes where they doe live, yet some of them for variety, will have the skinnes of such beasts that frequent the partes of their neighbors, which they purchase of them, by Commerce and Trade.

The Indians make good lether. These skinnes they convert into very good lether, making the same plume and soft. Some of these skinnes they dresse with the haire on, and some with the haire off; the hairy side in winter time they weare next their bodies, and in warme weather, they weare the haire outwardes: they make likewise some Coates of the Feathers of Turkies, which they weave together with twine of their owne makinge, very pritily: these garments they weare like mantels knit over their shoulders, and put under their arme: they have likewise another sort of mantels, made of Mose skinnes, which beast is a great large Deere, so bigge as a horse, these skinnes they commonly dresse bare, and make them wondrous white and stripe them with size, round about the borders, in forme like lace set on by a Taylor, and some they stripe with size, in workes of severall fashions very curious, according to the severall fantasies of the workemen, wherein they strive to excell one another: *Indians ingenious workemen for their garments.* And Mantels made of Beares skinnes is an usuall wearinge, among the Natives, that live where the Beares doe haunt: they make shooes of Mose skinnes, which is the principall leather used to that purpose; and for want of such lether (which is the strongest) they make shooes of Deeres skinnes, very handsomly and commodious, and of such deeres skinnes as they dresse bare, they make stockinges, that comes within their shooes, like a stirrop stockinge, and is fastned above at their belt which is about their middell; Every male after hee attaines unto the age, which they call Pubes, wereth a belt about his middell, and a broad peece of lether that goeth betweene his leggs, and is tuckt up both before and behinde under that belt, and this they weare to hide their secreats of nature; *The modesty of the Indian men.* which by no meanes they will suffer to be seene, so much modesty they use in that particular, those garments they allwayes put on, when they goe a huntinge to keepe their skinnes from the brush of the Shrubbs, and when they have their Apparrell one, they looke like Irish in their trouses, the Stockinges joyne so to their breeches. A good well growne deere skin is of great account with them, and it must have the tale on, or else they account it defaced, the tale being three times as long as the tales of our English Deere, yea foure times so longe, this when they travell is raped round about their body, and with a girdle of their making, bound round about their middles, to which girdle is fastned a bagg, in which his instruments be, with which hee can strike fire upon any occasion.

Thus with their bow in their left hand, and their quiver of Arrowes at their back, hanging one their left shoulder with the lower end of it, in their right hand, they will runne away a dogg trot, untill they come to their journey end, and in this kinde of ornament, (they doe seeme to me) to be hansomer, then when they are in English apparrell, their gesture being answerable to their one habit and not unto ours.

Indians travaile with materials to strike fire at all times.

Their women have shooes and stockinges to weare likewise when they please, such as the men have, but the mantle they use to cover their nakednesse with, is much longer then that, which the men use; for as the men have one Deeres skinn, the women have two soed together at the full lenght, and it is so lardge that it trailes after them, like a great Ladies trane, and in time I thinke they may have their Pages to beare them up: and where the men use but one Beares skinn for a Mantle, the women have two soed together; and if any of their women would at any time shift one, they take that which they intend to make use of, and cast it over them round, before they shifte away the other, for modesty, being unwilling to be seene to discover their nakednesse, and the one being so cast over they slip the other from under them in a decent manner, which is to be noted in people uncivilized, therein they seeme to have as much modesty as civilized people, and deserve to be applauded for it.

The Indians ashamed of their nakednesse.

Chap. VII.

Of their Child-bearing, and delivery, and what manner of persons they are.

THe women of this Country, are not suffered to be used for procreation, untill the ripenesse of their age, at which time they weare a redd cap made of lether in forme like to our flat caps, and this they weare for the space of 12 moneths: for all men to take notice of them that have any minde to a wife; and then it is the custome of some of their Sachems or Lords of the territories, to have the first say or maidenhead of the females? (very apt they are) to be with childe, and very laborious when they beare children, yea when they are as great as they can be, yet in that case they neither forbeare laboure, nor travaile, I have seene them in that plight with burthens at their

The women big with child very laborious.

backs enough to load a horse, yet doe they not miscarry, but have a faire delivery, and a quick, their women are very good midwifes, and the women very lusty after delivery and in a day or two will travell or trudge about. Their infants are borne with haire on their heads; and are of complexion white as our nation, but their mothers in their infancy make a bath of Wallnut leaves, huskes of Walnuts, and such things as will staine their skinne for ever, wherein they dip and washe them to make them tawny, the coloure of their haire is black, and their eyes black, these infants are carried at their mothers backs, by the help of a cradle made of a board forket at both ends, whereon the childe is fast bound, and wrapped in furres: his knees thrust up towards his bellie, because they may be the more usefull for them when he sitteth, which is as a dogge does on his bumme, and this cradle surely preserves them better then the cradles of our nation; for as much, as we finde them well proportioned not any of them, crooked backed or wry legged, and to give their charracter in a worde, they are as proper men and women for feature and limbes as can be found, for flesh and bloud as active: longe handed they are, (I never sawe a clunchfisted Salvadg amongst them all in my time.) The colour of their eies being so generally black, made a Salvage (that had a younge infant whose eies were gray,) shewed him to us and said they were English mens eies, I tould the Father, that his sonne was *nan weeteo*, which is a bastard, hee replied *titta Cheshetue squaa*, which is hee could not tell; his wife might play the whore and this child the father desired might have an English name, because of the likenesse of his eies which his father had in admiration, because of novelty amongst their Nation.

Children bathed to stain the skinne.

CHAP. VII.

Of their Reverence, and respect to age.

IT is a thing to be admired, and indeede made a president, that a Nation yet uncivilizied, should more respect age then some nations civilized; since there are so many precepts both of divine and humane writers extant: to instruct more Civill Nations in that particular wherein they excell, the younger are allwayes obedient unto the elder people, and at their commaunds in every respect without grummbling, in all councels (as therein they are cir-

Age honoured among the Indians.

cumspect to do their acciones by advise and councell and not rashly or inconsiderately, the younger mens opinion shall be heard, but the old mens opinion and councell imbraced and followed, besides as the elder feede and provide for the younger in infancy: so doe the younger after being growne to yeares of manhood, provide for those that be aged, and in distribution of Acctes the elder men are first served, by their dispensator and their counsels (especially if they be powahs) are esteemed as oracles amongst the younger Natives.

The consideration of these things, mee thinkes should reduce some of our irregular young people of civilized Nations: when this story shall come to their knowledge, to better manners, and make them ashamed of their former error in this kinde, and to become hereafter more duetyfull, which I as a friend (by observation having found) have herein recorded for that purpose.

CHAP. IX.

Of their pretty conjuring tricks.

IF we doe not judge amisse of these Salvages in accounting them witches, yet out of all question, we may be bould to conclude them to be but weake witches, such of them as wee call by the names of Powahs some correspondency they have with the Devil, out of al doubts as by some of their accions, in which they glory, is manifested Papasiquineo; that Sachem or Sagamore is a Powah of greate estimation amongst all kinde of Salvages, there hee is at their Revels (which is the time when a great company of Salvages meete, from severall parts of the Country, in amity with their neighbours) hath advaunced his honor in his feats or jugling tricks (as I may right tearme them) to the admiration of the spectators whome hee endevoured to perswade, that he would goe under water to the further side of a river to broade for any man to undertake with a breath, which thing hee performed by swimming over & deluding the company with casting a mist before their eies that see him enter in and come out, but no part of the way hee has bin seene, likewise by our English in the heat of all summer to make Ice appeare in a bowle of faire water, first having the water set before him hee hath begunne his incantation according to their usuall accustome and before the same has bin ended a thick Clowde has darkned the aire and on a sodane a thunder clap hath bin heard that has amazed the natives, in an instant hee hath shewed a firme peece of Ice to flote in the middest of the bowle in the presence of the vulgar people, which doubtles was done by the agility of Satan his consort.

And by meanes of these sleights and such like trivial things, as these they gain such estimation amongst the rest of the Salvages; that it is thought a very impious matter for any man to derogate from the words of these Powahs. In so much as hee that should slight them, is thought to commit a crime no lesse hainous amongst them, as sacriledge is with us, as may appeare by this one passage, which I wil set forth for an instance.

A Salvage entertained a factor.

A neighbour of mine that had entertain'd a Salvage into his service, to be his factor for the beaver trade amongst his countrymen, delivered unto him divers parcells of commodities, fit for them to trade with; amongst the rest there was one coate of more esteeme then any of the other, and with this his new entertained marchant man travels amongst his countrymen to truck them away for beaver: as our custome hath bin, the Salvage went up into the Country amongst his neighbours for beaver & returned with some, but not enough answerable to his Masters expectation, but being called to an accompt and especially for that one Cote of speciall note; made answer that he had given that coate to Tantoquineo, a Powah: to which his master in a rage cryed what have I to doe with Tantoquineo? The Salvage very angry at the matter cryed, what you speake; you are not a very good man, wil you not give Tantoq. a coat? whats this? as if he had offered *Tantoquineo*, the greatest indignity that could be devised: so great is the estimation and reverence that these people have of these Ingling Powahs, who are usually sent for (when any person is sicke and ill at ease) to recover them, for which they receive rewards as doe our Chirgeons and Phisitions, and they doe make a trade of it, and boast of their skill where they come: One amongst the rest did undertake to cure an Englishman of a swelling of his hand for a parcell of biskett, which being delivered him, hee tooke the party greived into the woods aside from company, and with the helpe of the devill (as may be conjectured,) quickly recovered him of that swelling, and sent him about his worke againe.

An Englishman cured of a swelling.

Chap. X.

Of their duels and the honourable estimation of victory obtained thereby.

THese Salvages are not apt to quarrell one with another: yet such hath bin the occasion that a difference hath happened, which hath growne to that height, that it has not bin reconciled otherwise then by combat, which hath bin performed in this manner, the two champions prepared the fight, with their bowes in hand, and a quiver full of arrowes at their backs, they have entered into the field, the Challenger and challenged have chosen two trees, standing within a little distance of each other; they have cast lotts for the cheife of the trees, then either champion setting himselfe behinde his tree watches an advantage, to let fly his shafts, and to gall his enemy, there they continue shooting at each other, if by chaunce they espie any part open, they endeavour to gall the combatant in that part; and use much agility in the performance of the taske they have in hand. Resolute they are in the execution of their vengeance, when once they have begunne, and will in no wise be daunted, or seeme to shrinck though they doe catch a clap with an arrow, but fight it out in this manner untill one or both be slaine.

How the Salvages performe theire duells.

I have bin shewed the places, where such duels have bin performed, and have found the trees marked for a memoriall of the Combat, where that champion hath stood, that had the hap to be slaine in the duell? and they count it the greatest honor that can be, to the serviving Cumbatant to shew the scares of the wounds, received in this kinde of Conflict, and if it happen to be on the arme as those parts are most in danger in these cases, they will alwayes were a bracelet upon that place of the arme, as a trophy of honor to their dying day.

Trees marked where they performe a duell.

Chap. XI.

Of the maintaining of their Reputation.

REputation is such a thing, that it keepes many men in awe, even amongst Civilized nations, and is very much stood upon it is (as one hath very well noted) the awe of great men and of Kings, and since I have observed it, to be maintained amongst Salvage people, I cannot chuse but give an instance thereof in this treatise, to confirme the common receaved opinion thereof.

The Sachem or Sagamore of Sagus made choise, (when hee came to mans estate) of a Lady of noble discent, Daughter to Papasiquineo: the Sachem or Sagamore of the territories neare Merrimack River a man of the best note and estimation in all those parts (and as my Countryman Mr. Wood declares in his prospect) a great Nigromancer, this Lady the younge Sachem with the consent & good liking of her father marries, and takes for his wife. Great entertainement, hee and his receaved in those parts at her fathers hands, where they weare fested in the best manner that might be expected, according to the Custome of their nation, with reveling, & such other solemnities as is usuall amongst them. The solemnity being ended, Papasiquineo causes a selected number of his men to waite upon his Daughter home: into those parts that did properly belong to her Lord, and husband, where the attendants had entertainment by the Sachem of Sagus and his Countrymen: the solemnity being ended, the attendants were gratified.

A marriage.

Not long after the new married Lady had a great desire to see her father, and her native country, from whence shee came, her Lord willing to pleasure her, & not deny her request (amongst them) thought to be reasonable commanded a selected number of his owne men to conduct his Lady to her Father; wherewith great respect they brought her: and having feasted there a while, returned to their owne country againe, leaving the Lady to continue there at her owne pleasure, amongst her friends, and old acquaintance: where shee passed away the time for a while: and in the end desired to returne to her Lord againe. Her father the old Papasiquineo having notice of her intent, sent some of his men on ambassage to the younge Sachem, his sonne in law, to let him understand that his daughter was not willing, to absent her selfe from his company any longer; & therefore (as the messengers had in charge) desired the younge Lord to send a convoy for her: but hee standing upon tearmes of honor, & the maintaining of his reputatiō, returned to his father in law this answere that when she departed from him, hee caused his men to waite upon her to her fathers territories, as it did become him: but now shee had an intent to returne, it did become her father, to send her back with a convoy of his own people: & that it stood not with his reputation to make himself or his men so servile, to fetch her againe. The old Sachem

An ambassage sent from Papasiquineo to his sone in law, a Sachem.

Papasiquineo having this message returned, was inraged? to think that his young son in law did not esteeme him at a higher rate, then to capitulate with him about the matter, & returne him this sharpe reply; that his daughters bloud, and birth deserved no more respect; then to be so slighted, & therefore if he would have her company, hee were best to send or come for her.

The younge Sachem not willing to under value himselfe, and being a man of a stout spirit, did not stick to say, that he should either send her, by his owne Convey, or keepe her; for hee was not determined to stoope so lowe.

So much these two Sachems stood upon tearmes of reputation with each other, the one would not send her, & the other would not send for her, leest it should be any diminishing of honor on his part, that should seeme to comply, that the Lady (when I came out of the Country) remained still with her father; which is a thinge worth the noting, that Salvage people should seeke to maintaine their reputation so much as they doe.

CHAP. XII.

Of their trafficke and trade one with another.

ALthough these people have not the use of navigation, whereby they may trafficke as other nations, that are civilized, use to doe, yet doe they barter for such commodities as they have, & have a kinde of beads in steede of money, to buy withall such things as they want, which they call Wampampeak: and it is of two sorts, the one is white, the other is of a violet coloure. These are made of the shells of fishe; the white with them is as silver with us; the other as our gould, and for these beads they buy, and sell, not onely amongst themselves, but even with us.

Beads instead of Money.

We have used to sell them any of our commodities for this Wampampeak, because we know, we can have beaver again of them for it: and these beads are currant in all the parts of New England, from one end of the Coast to the other.

The name of their beads Wimpanpeak.

And although some have indevoured by example to have the like made, of the same kinde of shels, yet none hath ever, as yet, attained to any perfection in the composure of them, but that the Salvages have found a great difference to be in the one and the other; and have knowne the counterfett beads from those of their owne making; and have, and doe slight them.

The skinnes of beasts are sould and bartered to such people, as have none of the same kinde in the parts where they live.

Likewise they have earthen potts of divers sizes, from a quarte to a gallon, 2. or 3. to boyle their vitels in; very stronge, though they be thin like our Iron potts.

They have dainty wooden bowles of maples, of highe price amongst them, and these are dispersed by bartering one with the other, and are but in certaine parts of the Country made, where the severall trades are appropriated to the inhabitants of those parts onely.

So likewise (at the season of the yeare) the Salvages that live by the Sea side for trade with the inlanders for fresh water, reles curious silver reles, which are bought up of such as have them not frequent in other places, chestnuts, and such like usefull things as one place affordeth, are sould to the inhabitants of another: where they are a novelty accompted amongst the natives of the land; and there is no such thing to barter withall, as is their Whampampeake.

Chap. XIII.

Of their Magazines or Storehowses.

What care they take to lay up corne for winter.

THese people are not without providence, though they be uncivilized, but are carefull to preserve foede in store against winter, which is the corne that they laboure and dresse in the summer, And although they eate freely of it, whiles it is growinge, yet have they a care to keepe a convenient portion thereof; to releeve them in the dead of winter, (like to the Ant and the Bee) which they put under ground.

Their Barnes are holes made in the earth, that will hold a Hogshead of corne a peece in them. In these (when their corne is out of the huske and well dried) they lay their store in greate baskets (which they make of Sparke) with matts under about the sides and on the top: and putting it into the place made for it, they cover it with earth: and in this manner it is preserved from destruction or putrifaction; to be used in case of necessity, and not else.

And I am perswaded, that if they knew the benefit of Salte

(as they may in time,) and the meanes to make salte meate fresh againe, they would endeaver to preserve fishe for winter, as well as corne; and that if any thinge bring them to civility, it will be the use of Salte, to have foode in store, which is a cheife benefit in a civilized Commonwealth.

These people have begunne already to incline to the use of Salte. Many of them would begge Salte of mee for to carry home with them, that had frequented our howses and had been acquainted with our Salte meats: and Salte I willingly gave them; although I sould them all things else: onely because they should be delighted with the use there of; and thinke it a commodity of no value in it selfe, although the benefit was great, that might be had by the use of it.

They begg Salte of the English.

Chap. XIV.

Of theire Subtilety.

These people are not (as some have thought a dull, or slender witted people; but very ingenious and very subtile. I could give maine instances to maintaine mine opinion of them in this: But I will onely relate one, which is a passage worthy to be observed.

In the Massachusetts bay lived Cheecatawback the Sachem or Sagamore of those territories, who had large dominions, which hee did appropriate to himselfe.

Into those parts came a greate company of Salvages, from the territories of Narohiganset, to the number of 100. persons; and in this Sachems Dominions they intended to winter.

When they went a hunting for turkies: they spreade over such a greate scope of ground, that a Turkie could hardly escape them: Deare they killed up in greate abundance, and feasted their bodies very plentifully: Beavers they killed by no allowance: the skinnes of those they traded away at wassaguscus with my neighboures for corne, and such other commodities as they had neede of; and my neighboures had a wonderfull great benefit by their being in those parts. Yea sometimes (like genious fellowes) they would present their Marchant with a fatt beaver skinne, alwayes the tayle was not diminished, but presented full and whole: although the tayle is a present for a Sachem, and is of such masculaine vertue, that if some of our Ladies knew the benefit thereof

They trade away beaver skinnes for corne.

A beaver skinne with his tayle on of great estimacion.

they would desire to have ships sent of purpose, to trade for the tayle alone, it is such a rarity, as is not more esteemed of then reason doth require.

But the Sachem Cheecatawbak (on whose possessions they usurped, and converted the commodities thereof to their owne use, contrary to his likeing) not being of power to resist them, practised to doe it by a subtile stratagem. And to that end gave it out amongst us, that the cause why these other Salvages of the Narohigansets, came into these parts, was to see what strength we were of, and to watch an opportunity to cut us off, and take that which they found in our custody usefull for them; And added further, they would burne our howses, and that they had caught one of his men, named Meshebro, and compelled him to discover to them where their barnes, Magazines, or storehowses were, and had taken away his corne, and seemed to be in a pittifull perplexity about the matter.

A subtle plot of a Sachem.

And the more to adde reputation to this tale, desires that his wifes and children might be harbered in one of our howses. This was graunted, and my neighbours put on corslets, head-peeces, and weapons defensive and offensive.

This thing being knowne to Cheecatawback, hee caused some of his men to bring the Narohigansets to trade, that they might see the preparation.

The Salvage that was a stranger to the plott, simply comming to trade, and finding his merchants, lookes like lobsters, all cladd in harnesse, was in a maze to thinke what would be the end of it. Haste hee made to trade away his furres, and tooke any thing for them, wishing himselfe well rid of them, and of the company in the howse.

A Salvage scared.

But (as the manner has bin) hee must eate some furmety before hee goe: downe hee sits, and eats, and withall had an eie on every side; and now and then saw a sword, or a dagger layd a thwart a headpeece, which hee wondered at, and asked his guide whether the company were not angry. The guide, (that was privy to his Lords plot) answered in his language, that hee could not tell. But the harmelesse Salvage before hee had halfe filled his belly, started up on a sodayne, and ranne out of the howse in such hast, that hee left his furmety there, and stayed not to looke behinde him who came after: Glad hee was that he had escaped so.

The subtle Sachem hee playd the tragedian; and fained a feare of being surprised; and sent to see whether the enemies (as the Messenger termed them) were not in the howse; and comes in a by way with his wifes and children; and stopps the chinkes of the out howse, for feare the fire might be seene in the night, and be a meanes to direct his enemies where to finde them.

And in the meane time, hee prepared for his Ambassador to his enemies a Salvage, that had lived 12. moneths in England, to the end it might adde reputation to his ambassage. This man hee sends to those intruding Narohigansets, to tell them that they did very great injury, to his Lord, to trench upon his prerogatives: and advised them to put up their pipes, and begon in time: if they would not, that his Lord would come upon them, and in his ayd his freinds the English, who were up in armes already to take his part, and compell them by force to be gone, if they refused to depart by faire meanes.

A Salvage that had lived 12. Moneths in England, sent for an Ambassador.

This message comming on the neck of that which doubtlesse the fearefull Salvage had before related of his escape, and what hee had observed; caused all those hundred Narohigansets (that meant us no hurt) to be gone with bagg, and baggage, And my neighboures were gulled by the subtilety of this Sachem, and lost the best trade of beaver that ever they had for the time, and in the end found theire error in this kinde of credulity when it was too late.

A good opportunity of traffick lost by the subtility of a Sachem.

Chap. XV.

Of their admirable perfection, in the use of the sences.

THis is a thinge not onely observed by mee, and diverse of the Salvages of New England, but also, by the French men in Nova Francia, and therefore I am the more incouraged to publish in this Treatice my observation of them, in the use of theire sences: which is a thinge that I should not easily have bin induced, to beleeve, if I my selfe, had not bin an eie witnesse, of what I shall relate.

I have observed, that the Salvages have the sence of seeing so farre beyond any of our Nation, that one would allmost beleeve they had intelligence of the Devill, sometimes: when they have tould us of a shipp at Sea, which they have seene, soener by one hower, yea two howers sayle, then any English man that stood by; of purpose to looke out, their sight is so excellent.

The Salvages have the sence of seeinge better then the English.

Their eies indeede are black as iett; and that coler is accounted the strongest for sight. And as they excell us in this particular so much noted, so I thinke they excell us in all the rest.

This I am sure, I have well observed, that in the sence of smelling, they have very great perfection which is confirmed by the opinion of the French, that are planted about Canada, who have made relation, That they are so perfect in the use of that sence, that they will distinguish between a Spaniard and a Frenchman by the sent of the hand onely. And I am perswaded, that the Author of this Relation has seene very probable reasons, that have induced him, to be of that opinion; and I am the more willing to give credit thereunto, because I have observed in them so much, as that comes to.

Salvages that will distinguish a Spaniard from a frenchman by the smell of the hand.

I have seene a Deare passe by me upon a neck of Land, and a Salvage that has pursued him by the view.

I have accompanied him in this pursuite; and the Salvage, pricking the Deare, comes where hee findes the view of two deares together, leading several wayes. One hee was sure, was fresh, but which (by the sence of seeing) hee could not judge, therefore, with his knife, hee diggs up the earth of one; and by smelling, sayes, that was not of the fresh Deare: then diggs hee up the other; and viewing and smelling to that, concludes it to be the view of the fresh Deare, which hee had pursued, and thereby followes the chase and killes that Deare, and I did eate part of it with him: such is their perfection in these two sences.

A Deare pursued by the view of the foote, hee was found and killed.

CHAP. XVI.

Of their acknowledgment of the Creation, and immortality of the Soule.

ALthough these Salvages are found to be without Religion, Law, and King (as Sir William Alexander hath well observed,) yet are they not altogether without the knowledge of God (historically) for they have it amongst them by tradition, that God made one man and one woman, and bad them live together, and get children, kill deare, beasts, birds, fish, and fowle, and what they would at their pleasure; and that their posterity was full of evill, and made God so angry: that hee let in the Sea upon them, & drowned the greatest part of them, that were naughty men, (the Lord destroyed so.)

And they went to Sanaconquam who feeds upon them, pointing to the Center of the Earth: where they imagine is the habitation of the Devill:) the other, (which were not destroyed,) increased the world; and when they died (because they were good) went to the howse of Kytan, pointing to the setting of the sonne; where they eate all manner of dainties, and never take paines (as now) to provide it.

The beleefe of the Salvages.

Kytan makes provision (they say) and saves them that laboure and there they shall live with him forever voyd of care. And they are perswaded that Kytan is hee that makes corne growe, trees growe, and all manner of fruits.

The Sonne called Kytan.

And that wee that use the booke of Common prayer, doo it to declare to them, that cannot reade, what Kytan has commanded us, and that wee doe pray to him with the helpe of that booke; and doe make so much accompt of it, that a Salvage (who had lived in my howse before hee had taken a wife, by whome hee had children) made this request to mee (knowing that I allwayes used him with much more respect than others.) That I would let his sonne be brought up in my howse, that hee might be taught to reade in that booke: which request of his I granted; and hee was a very joyfull man to thinke, that his sonne should thereby (as hee said) become an Englishman; and then hee would be a good man.

A Salvage desired to have his sonn brought up to learne the booke of common prayer.

I asked him who was a good man; his answere was, hee that would not lye, nor steale.

These, with them, are all the capitall crimes, that can be imagined; all other are nothing in respect of those; and hee that is free from these, must live with Kytan for ever, in all manner of pleasure.

Chap. XVII.

Of their Annals and funerals.

THese people, that have by tradition some touch of the immortality of the soule, have likewise a custome to make some monuments, over the place where the corps is interred: But they put a greate

Their custom in burryinge.

difference betweene persons of noble, and of ignoble, or obscure, or inferior discent. For indeed in the grave of the more noble, they put a planck in the bottom for the corps to be layed upon and on each side a plancke, and a plancke upon the top in forme of a chest, before they cover the place with earth. This done, they erect some thing over the grave in forme of a hearse cloath, as was that of Cheekatawbacks mother, which the Plimouth planters defaced, because they accounted it an act of superstition. Which did breede a brawle as hath bin before related: for they hold impious, and inhumane: to deface the monuments of the dead. They themselves esteeme of it as piaculum, and have a custome amongst them, to keepe their annals: & come at certaine times to lament, & bewaile the losse of their freind; & use to black their faces, which they so weare in stead of a mourning ornament for a longer or a shorter time, according to the dignity of the person: so is their annals kept and observed with their accustomed solemnity. Afterwards they absolutely abandon the place, because they suppose the sight thereof, will but renew their sorrow.

Their manner of Monuments.

At burrials, they black their faces.

It was a thing very offensive to them, at our first comming into those parts, to aske of them for any one that had bin dead; but of later times it is not so offensively taken, to renew the memory of any deseased person, because by our example (which they are apt to followe) it is made more familiare unto them; and they marvell to see no monuments over our dead, and therefore thinke no great Sachem is yet come into those parts: or not as yet deade, because they see the graves all alike.

Chap. XVIII.

Of their Custome in burning the Country, and the reason thereof.

THe Salvages are accustomed, to set fire of the Country in all places where they come; and to burne it, twize a yeare, vixe at the Spring, and the fall of the leafe. The reason that mooves them to doe so, is because it would other wise be so overgrowne with underweedes, that it would be all a copice wood, and the people would not be able in any wise to passe through the Country out of a beaten path.

The Salvages fire the Country twice a yeare.

The meanes that they do it with, is with certaine minerall stones, that they carry about them: in baggs made for that purpose of the skinnes of little beastes which they convert into good lether; carrying in the same a peece of touch wood (very excellent for that purpose of their owne making. These minnerall stones they have from the Piquenteenes (which is to the Southward of all the plantations in New England) by trade and trafficke with those people.

The burning of the grasse destroyes the underwoods, and so scorcheth the elder trees, that it shrinkes them, and hinders their grouth very much: So that hee that will looke to finde large trees, and good tymber, must not depend upon the help, of a woodden prospect to finde them on the upland ground; but must seeke for them, (as I and others have done) in the lower grounds where the grounds are wett when the Country is fired: by reason of the snow water that remaines there for a time, untill the Sunne by continuance of that hath exhaled the vapoures of the earth, and dried up those places, where the fire (by reason of the moisture) can have no power to doe them any hurt: and if he would endevoure to finde out any goodly Cedars, hee must not seeke for them on the higher grounds, but make his inquest for them in the vallies, for the Salvages by this Custome of theirs, have spoiled all the rest: for this custome hath bin continued from the beginninge.

And least their firing of the Country in this manner; should be an occasion of damnifying us, and indaingering our habitations; wee our selves have used carefully about the same times; to observe the winds and fire the grounds about our owne habitations, to prevent the Dammage that might happen by any neglect thereof, if the fire should come neere those howses in our absence.

For when the fire is once kindled, it dilates and spreads it selfe as well against, as with the winde; burning continually night and day, untill a shower of raine falls to quench it.

And this custome of firing the Country is the meanes to make it passable, and by that meanes the trees growe here, and there as in our parks: and makes the Country very beautifull, and commodious.

Chap. XIX.

Of their inclination to Drunkenesse.

ALthough Drunkennesse be justly termed a vice, which the Salvages are ignorant of, yet the benefit is very great that comes to the planters by the sale of strong liquor to the Salvages, who are much taken with the delight of it, for they will pawne their wits, to purchase the acquaintance of it, yet in al the cōmerce that I had with them, I never proffered them any such thing; nay I would hardly let any of them have a drame unless hee were a Sachem, or a Winnaytue, that is a rich man, or a man of estimation, next in degree to a Sachem, or Sagamore: I alwayes tould them it was amongst us the Sachems drinke. But they say if I come to the Northerne parts of the Country, I shall have no trade, if I will not supply thē with lusty liquors, it is the life of the trade, in all those parts, for it so happened, that thus a Salvage desperately killed himselfe, when hee was drunke, a gunne being charged and the cock up, hee sets the mouth to his brest, and putting back the tricker with his foote, shot himselfe dead.

Chap. XX.

That the Salvages live a contended life.

A Gentleman and a traveller, that had bin in the parts of New England for a time, when hee retorned againe in his discourse of the Country, wondered (as hee said,) that the natives of the land lived so poorely, in so rich a Country, like to our Beggers in England: Surely that Gentleman had not time or leasure whiles hee was there, truely to informe himselfe of the state of that Country, and the happy life the Salvages would leade weare they once brought to Christianity.

The Salvages want the art of navigation.

I must confesse they want the use and benefit of Navigation (which is the very sinnus of a flourishing Commonwealth,) yet are they supplied with all manner of needfull things, for the maintenance of life and lifelyhood, Foode and rayment are the cheife of all that we make true use of; and of these they finde no want, but have, them in a most plentifull manner.

If our beggers of England should with so much ease (as they,) furnish themselves with foode, at all seasons, there would not be so many starved in the streets, neither would so many gaoles be stuffed, or gallouses furnished with poore wretches, as I have seene them.

But they of this sort of our owne nation, that are fitt to goe to this Canaan are not able to transport themselves, and most of them unwilling to goe from the good ale tap; which is the very loadstone of the lande by which our English beggers steere theire Course: it is the Northpole to which the flowre-deluce of their compasse points; the more is the pitty that the Commonalty of oure Land are of such leaden capacities, as to neglect so brave a Country, that doth so plentifully feede Maine lusty and a brave, able men, women, and children that have not the meanes that a Civilized Nation hath to purchase foode and rayment: which that Country with a little industry will yeeld a man in a very comfortable measure; without overmuch carking.

I cannot deny but a civilized Nation, hath the preheminence of an uncivilized, by meanes of those instruments that are found to be common amongst civile people, and the uncivile want the use of, to make themselves masters of those ornaments, that make such a glorious shew, that will give a man occasion to cry, *sic transit gloria Mundi.*

Now since it is but foode and rayment that men that live needeth (though not all alike,) why should not the Natives of New England be sayd to live richly having no want of either: Cloaths are the badge of sinne, and the more variety of fashions is but the greater abuse of the Creature, the beasts of the forrest there doe serve to furnish them at any time, when they please: fish and flesh they have in greate abundance which they both roast and boyle.

They are indeed not served in dishes of plate with variety of Sauces to procure appetite, that needs not there. The rarity of the aire begot by the medicinable quality of the sweete herbes of the Country, alwayes procures good stomakes to the inhabitants.

I must needs commend them in this particular, that though they buy many commodities of our Nation, yet they keepe but fewe, and those of speciall use.

They love not to bee cumbered with many utensilles, and although every proprietor knowes his owne, yet all things (so long as they will last,) are used in common amongst them: A bisket cake given to one; that one breakes it equally into so many parts, as there be persons in his company, and distributes it. Platoes Commonwealth is so much practised by these people.

They leade a happy life, being voyd of care.

According to humane reason guided onely by the light of nature, these people leades the more happy and freer life, being voyde of care, which torments the mindes of so many Christians: Theyare not delighted in baubles, but in usefull things.

Their naturall drinke is of the Christall fountaine, and this they take up in their hands, by joyning them close together. They take up a great quantity at a time, and drinke at the wrists, It was the sight of such a feate, which made Diogenes hurle away his dishe, and like one that would have this principall confirmed. *Natura paucis contentat*, used a dish no more.

They make use of ordinary things, one of anothers as common.

I have observed that they will not be troubled with superfluous commodities. Such things as they finde, they are taught by necessity to make use of they will make choise of; and seeke to purchase with industry so that in respect, that their life is so voyd of care, and they are so loving also that they make use of those things they enjoy (the wife onely excepted) as common goods, and are therein, so compassionate that rather than one should starve through want, they would starve all, thus doe they passe away the time merrily, not regarding our pompe (which they see dayly before their faces) but are better content with their owne, which some men esteeme so meanely of.

They may be rather accompted to live richly wanting nothing that is needefull; and to be commended for leading a contented life, the younger being ruled by the Elder, and the Elder ruled by the Powahs, and the Powahs are ruled by the Devill, and then you may imagin what good rule is like to be amongst them.

F I N I S.

NEW ENGLISH CANAAN, OR NEW CANAAN.

The Second Booke.

Containing a description of the bewty of the Country with her naturall indowements, both in the Land and Sea, with the great Lake of Erocoise.

CHAP. I

The generall Survey of the Country.

IN the Moneth of Iune, Anno Salutis: 1622. It was my chaunce to arrive in the parts of New England with 30. Servants, and provision of all sorts fit for a plantation: And whiles our howses were building, I did endeavour to take a survey of the Country: The more I looked, the more I liked it.

And when I had more seriously considered of the bewty of the place, with all her faire indowments, I did not thinke that in all the knowne world it could be paralel'd. For so many goodly groues of trees; dainty fine round rising hillucks: delicate faire large plaines,

A famous Country.

Their fountaines are as cleare as Christall. sweete cristall fountaines, and cleare running streames, that twine in fine meanders through the meads, making so sweete a murmering noise to heare, as would even lull the sences with delight a sleepe, so pleasantly doe, they glide upon the pebble stones, jetting most jocundly where they doe meete; and hand in hand runne downe to Neptunes Court, to pay the yearely tribute, which they owe to him as soveraigne Lord of all the springs. Contained within the volume of the Land, Fowles in *Greate store of fowles, fish and turtledoves.* abundance, Fish in multitude, and discovered besides; Millions of Turtledoves one the greene boughes: which sate pecking, of the full ripe pleasant grapes, that were supported by the lusty trees, whose fruitfull loade did cause the armes to bend, which here and there dispersed (you might see) Lillies and of the Daphneantree, which made the Land to mee seeme paradice, for in mine eie, t'was Natures Master-peece: Her cheifest Magazine of, all where lives her store: if this Land be not rich, then is the whole world poore.

What I had resolved on, I have really performed, and I have endeavoured, to use this abstract as an instrument, to bee the meanes, to communicate the knowledge which I have gathered, by my many yeares residence in those parts, unto my Countrymen, to the end, that they may the better perceive their error, who cannot imagine, that there is any Country in the universall world, which may be compared unto our native soyle, I will now discover unto them a Country whose indowments are by learned men allowed to stand in a paralell with the Israelites Canaan, which none will deny, to be a land farre more excellent then Old England in her proper nature.

This I consider I am bound in duety (as becommeth a Christian man) to performe, for the glory of God, in the first place; next (according to Cicero,) to acknowledge that, *Non nobis solum nati sumus, sed partim patria, partim parentes, partim amici vindicant.*

For which cause I must approove of the indeavoures of my Country men, that have bin studious to inlarge the territories of his Majesties empire by planting Colonies in America.

And of all other I must applaude the judgement of those that have made choise of this part (whereof I now treat) being of all other most absolute, as I will make it appeare, hereafter by way of paralell, among those that have setled themselves in new England, some have gone for their conscience sake, (as they professe,) & I wish that they may plant the Gospel of Iesus Christ: as becommeth them, sincerely and without satisme or faction, whatsoever their former or present practises are (which I intend not to justifie, howsoever they have deserved (in mine opinion) some commendationes, in that they have furnished the Country, so commodiously in so short a time, although it hath bin but for their owne profit, yet posterity will taste the sweetnes of it and that very sodainly.

And since my taske in this part of mine abstract, is to intreat of the naturall indowments, of the Country, I will make a breife demonstration of them in order, severally, according to their severall qualities: and shew you what they are, and what profitable use may be made of them by industry.

CHAP. II.

What trees are there and how commodious.

OAkes are there of two sorts, white and redd, excellent tymber for the building, both of howses, and shipping: and they are found to be a tymber, that is more tough then the oak of England. They are excellent for pipe-staves and such like vessels; and pipe-staves at the Canary Ilands are a prime commodity, I have knowne them there at 35. p. the 1000, and will purchase a fraight of wines there before any commodity in England, their onely wood being pine, of which they are enforced, also to build shippinge; of oackes there is great abundance in the parts of New England, and they may have a prime place in the Catalogue of commodities. 1. *Oake.*

Ashe there is store and very good for staves, oares or pipes, and may have a place in the same Catalogue. 2. *Ashe.*

Elme: of this sort of trees, there are some; but there hath not as yet bin found any quantity to speake of. 3. *Elme.*

Beech there is of two sorts, redd and white very excellent for trenchers, or chaires and also for oares and may be accompted for a commodity. 4. *Beech.*

Wallnutt, of this sorte of wood there is infinite store and there are 4 sorts, it is an excellent wood, for many uses approoved, the younger trees are imployed for hoopes, and are the best for that imployement of all other stuffe whatsoever, the Nutts serve when they fall to feede our swine, 5. *Walnutt.*

which make them the delicatest bacon of all other foode, and is therein a cheife commodity.

6. *Chestnuts.* Chestnutt, of this sorte there is very greate plenty; the tymber whereof is excellent for building and is a very good commodity, especially in respect of the fruit, both for man and beast.

7. *Pine.* Pine, of this sorte there is infinite store in some parts of the Country. I have travelled 10. miles together, where is little, or no other wood growing. And of these may be made rosin, pitch, and tarre, which are such usefull commodities, that if wee had them not from other Countries in Amity with England, our Navigation would decline. Then how great the commodity of it will be to our Nation, to have it of our owne, let any man judge.

8. *Cedar.* Cedar, of this sorte there is abundaunce; and this wood was such as Salomon used for the building of that glorious Temple at Hierusalem, and there are of these Cedars, firre trees, and other materialls necessary for the building of many faire Temples, if there were any Salomons to be at the Cost of them, and if any man be desirous to finde out in what part of the Country the best Cedars are, he must get into the bottom grounds, and in vallies that are wet at the spring of the yeare, where the moisture preserves them from the fire in spring time and not in a wooden prospect, This wood cutts red, and is good for bedsteads tables and chests, and may be placed in the Catalogue of Commodities.

9. *Cypres.* Cypres, of this there is great plenty, and vulgarly this tree hath bin taken, for another sort of Cedar; but workemen put a difference betweene this Cypres, and the Cedar, especially in the colour; for this is white and that redd white and likewise in the finenes of the leafe and the smoothnes of the barque. This wood is also sweeter then Cedar and (as it is in Garrets herball) a more bewtifull tree; it is of all other to my minde, most bewtifull, and cannot be denied to passe for a commodity.

10. *Spruce.* Spruce, of these there are infinite store, especially in the Northerne parts of the Country; and they have bin approoved by workemen in England, to be more tough, then those that they have out of the east country: from whence wee have them for masts and yards of shippes.

The Spruce of this Country are found to be 3. & 4. fadum aboute. The Spruce of this country are found to be 3. and 4. fadum about: and are reputed able single, to make masts for the biggest ship, that sayles on the maine Ocean, without peesing, which is more than the East country can afford. And seeing that Navigation is the very sinneus of a flourishing Commonwealth, it is fitting, to allow the Spruce tree a principall place, in the Catalogue of commodities.

Alder, of this sorte there is plenty by rivers sides good for turners. 11. *Alder.*

Birch, of this there is plenty in divers parts of the Country. Of the barck of these the Salvages of the Northerne parts make them delicate Canowes, so light, that two men will transport one of them over Land whether they list, and one of them will transporte tenne or twelve Salvages by water at a time. 12. *Birch.*

Mayple, of those trees there is greate abundance and these are very excellent, for bowles. The Indians use of it to that purpose, and is to be accompted a good commodity. 13. *Maple.*

Elderne, there is plenty in that Country, of this The Salvages make their Arrowes, and it hath no strong unsavery sent like our Eldern in England. 14. *Elderne.*

Hawthorne, of this there is two sorts, one of which beares a well tasting berry, as bigg as ones thumbe, and lookes like little Queene apples. 15. *Hawthorne.*

Vines, of this kinde of trees, there are that beare grapes of three colours, that is to say: white black, and red. 16. *Vines.*

The Country is so apt for vines, that (but for the fire at the spring of the yeare) the vines would so over spreade the land, that one should not be able to passe for them, the fruit is as bigg of some; as a musket bullet, and is excellent in taste.

Plumtrees, of this kinde there are many; some that beare fruit as bigg as our ordinary bullis: others there be, that doe beare fruite much bigger than peare plummes, their colour redd, and their stones flat, very delitious in taste. 17. *Plummes.*

Cheritrees, there are abundance, but the fruit is as small as our sloes, but if any of them were replanted, & grafted, in an orchard they would soone be raised by meanes of such and the like fruits. 18. *Cherries.*

There is greate abundance of Muske Roses in divers places: the water distilled excelleth our Rosewater of England. 19. *Roses.*

There is abundance of Sassafras and Sarsaperilla, growing in divers places of the land; whose budds at the spring doe perfume the aire. 20. 21. *Sassafras and Sarsaperilla.*

Other trees there are not greatly materiall to be recited in this abstract, as goose berries, rasberies, and other beries.

There is Hempe that naturally groweth, finer then our Hempe of England.

Chap. III.

Potthearbes and other herbes for Sallets.

THe Country there naturally affordeth very good potherbes and sallet herbes and those of a more maskuline vertue then any of the same species in England; as Potmarioram, Tyme, Alexander, Angellica, Pursland, Violets, and Anniseeds, in very great abundance: and for the pott I gathered in summer, dried and crumbled into a bagg to preserve for winter store.

Potmarioram, Tyme, Alexander, Angellica, Pursland, Violets and Anniseeds.

Hunnisuckles, balme, and divers other good herbes are there, that grow without the industry of man, that are used when occasion serveth very commodiously.

Hunnisuckles and Balme.

Chap. IV.

Of Birds, and fethered fowles.

NOw that I have breifly shewed the Commodity of the trees, herbes, and fruits, I will shew you a description of the fowles of the aire, as most proper in ordinary course.

Swannes.

And first of the Swanne, because she is the biggest of all the fowles of that Country. There are of them in Merrimack River, and in other parts of the country, greate store at the seasons of the yeare.

The flesh is not much desired of the inhabitants, but the skinnes may be accompted a commodity, fitt for divers uses, both for fethers, and quiles.

Geese, pide, white, and gray.

There are Gesse of three sorts vize brant Geese, which are pide, and white Geese which are bigger, and gray Geese which are as bigg and bigger then the tame Geese of England, with black legges, black bills, heads, and necks black; the flesh farre more excellent, then the

Geese of England, wild or tame, yet the purity of the aire is such, that the biggest is accompted but an indifferent meale for a couple of men. There is of them great abundance. I have had often 1000. before the mouth of my gunne, I never saw any in England for my part so fatt, as I have killed there in those parts, the fethers of them makes a bedd, softer then any down bed that I have lyen on: and is there a very good commodity, the fethers of the Geese that I have killed in a short time, have paid for all the powther and shott, I have spent in a yeare, and I have fed my doggs with as fatt Geese there, as I have euer fed upon my selfe in England.

Fethers pay for powther and shot.

Ducks, there are of three kindes, pide Ducks, gray Ducks, and black Ducks in greate abundance: the most about my habitation were black Ducks: and it was a noted Custome at my howse, to have every mans Duck upon a trencher, and then you will thinke a man was not hardly used, they are bigger boddied, then the tame Ducks of England: very fatt and dainty flesh.

Ducks pide, gray, and black.

The common doggs fees were the gibletts, unlesse they were boyled now and than for to make broath.

Teales, there are of two sorts greene winged, and blew winged: but a dainty bird, I have bin much delighted with a rost of these for a second course, I had plenty in the rivers and ponds about my howse.

Teales greene and blew.

Widggens there are, and abundance of other water foule, some such as I have seene, and such as I have not seene else where, before I came into those parts, which are little regarded.

Widggens.

Simpes, there are like our Simpes in all respects, with very litle difference. I have shot at them onely, to see what difference I could finde betweene them and those of my native Country, and more I did not regard them.

Simpes.

Sanderlings are dainty bird, more full bodied than a Snipe, and I was much delighted to feede on them, because they were fatt, and easie to come by, because I went but a stepp or to for them: and I have killed betweene foure and five dozen at a shoot which would loade me home.

Sanderlings.

Their foode is at ebbing water on the sands, of small seeds, that grows on weeds there, and are very good pastime in August.

Cranes, there are greate store, that ever more came there at S. Davids day, and not before: that day they never would misse.

Cranes.

These sometimes eate our corne, and doe pay for their presumption well enough; and serveth there in powther, with turnips to supply the place of powthered beefe, and is a goodly bird in a dishe, and no discommodity.

Turkies. Turkies there are, which divers times in great flocks have sallied by our doores; and then a gunne (being commonly in a redinesse,) salutes them with such a courtesie, as makes them take a turne in the Cooke roome. They daunce by the doore so well.

Of these there hath bin killed, that have weighed forty eight pound a peece.

They are by mainy degrees sweeter then the tame Turkies of England, feede them how you can.

I had a Salvage who hath taken out his boy in a morning, and they have brought home their loades about noone.

I have asked them what number they found in the woods, who have answered Neent Metawna, which is a thousand that day; the plenty of them is such in those parts. They are easily killed at rooste, because the one being killed, the other sit fast neverthelesse, and this is no bad commodity.

Pheisants. There are a kinde of fowles which are commonly called Pheisants, but whether they be pheysants or no, I will not take upon mee, to determine. They are in forme like our pheisant henne of England. Both the male and the female are alike; but they are rough footed: and have stareing fethers about the head and neck, the body is as bigg as the pheysant henne of England; and are excellent white flesh, and delicate white meate, yet we seldome bestowe a shoote at them.

Partridges bigger in body as those of England. Partridges, there are much, like our Partridges of England, they are of the same plumes, but bigger in body. They have not the signe of the horse-shoe on the brest as the Partridges of England; nor are they coloured about the heads as those are; they sit on the trees. For I have seene 40. in one tree at a time: yet at night they fall on the ground, and sit until morning so together; and are dainty flesh.

Quailes bigger in body as those in England. There are quailes also, but bigger then the quailes in England. They take trees also: for I have numbered 60. upon a tree at a time. The cocks doe call at the time of the yeare, but with a different note from the cock quailes of England.

The Larkes sing not. The Larkes there, are like our Larkes of England in all respects: sauing that they do not use to sing at all.

There are Owles of divers kindes: but I did never heare any of them whop as ours doe. *Owles.*

There are Crowes, kights and rooks that doe differ in some respects from those of England. The Crowes (which I have much admired, what should be the cause) both smell and taste of Muske in summer, but not in winter. *The Crowes smell & tast of Muske in summer, but not in winter.*

There are Hawkes in New England of 5. sorts, and these of all other fether fowles I must not omitt, to speake of, nor neede I to make any Apology for my selfe, concerning any trespass, that I am like to make upon my judgement, concerning the nature of them, having bin bred in so genious a way, that I had the common use of them in England: and at my first arrivall in those parts practised to take a Lannaret, which I reclaimed, trained, and made flying in a fortnight, the same being a passinger at Michuelmas. I found that these are most excellent Mettell, rank winged, well conditioned, and not tickleish footed, and having whoods, bels, luers, and all things fitting, was desirous to make experiment of that kinde of Hawke, before any other. *Hawkes of five sorts.* *A Lanneret.*

And I am perswaded: that Nature hath ordained them to be of a farre better kinde, then any that have bin used in England. They have neither dorre, nor worm to feed upon (as in other parts of the world) the Country affording none, the use whereof in other parts, makes the Lannars there more bussardly then they be in New England.

There are likewise Fawcons, and tassell gentles, admirable well shaped birds, and they will tower up when they purpose to pray, and on a sodaine, when they esspie their game, they will make such a cancellere, that one would admire to behold them, Some there are more black, then any that have bin used in England. *Fawcons.*

The Tassell gent, (but of the least size) is an ornament for a person of estimation among the Indians to weare in the knot of his lock, with the traine upright, the body dried and stretched out. They take a great pride in the wearing of such an ornament, and give to one of us (that shall kill them one for that purpose) so much beaver as is worth three pounds sterling very willingly.

These doe us but little trespas, because they pray on such birds as are by the Sea side, and not on our Chickens. Goshawkes there are, and Tassels.

The Tassels are short trussed bussards; but the Goshawkes are well shaped, but they are small; *Goshawkes well shaped.*

some of white male, and some redd male, I have seene one with 8. barres in the traine. These fall on our bigger poultry: the lesser chicken. I thinke they scorne to make their pray of; for commonly the Cocke goes to wrack. Of these I have seene many, and if they come to trespasse me, I lay the law to them with the gunne, and take them dammage fesant.

Marlins small and greate.

There are very many Marlins; some very small, and some so large as is the Barbary Tassell.

I have often beheld these pretty birds, how they have scoured after the black bird, which is a small sized Choffe that eateth the Indian maisze.

Sparhawkes.

Sparhawkes there are also, the fairest, and best, shaped birds that I have ever beheld of that kinde, those that are litle, no use is made of any of them, neither are they regarded, I onely tried conclusions with a Lannaret at first comming; and when I found, what was in that bird, I turned him going: but for so much as I have observed of those birds, they may be a fitt present for a prince; and for goodnesse too be preferred before the Barbary, or any other used in Christendome, and especially the Lannars and Lannarets.

A Hunning bird, is as small as a Beetle. His bill as sharp as a needle point, and his fethers like silke.

There is a curious bird to see to, called a hunning bird, no bigger then a great Beetle; that out of question lives upon the Bee, which he eateth and catcheth amongst Flowers: For it is his Custome to frequent those places, Flowers hee cannot feed upon by reason of his sharp bill, which is like the poynt of a Spanish needle, but shorte. His fethers have a glasse like silke, and as hee stirres, they show to be of a chaingable coloure: and has bin, and is admired for shape coloure, and size.

CHAP. V.

Of the Beasts, of the forrest.

NOw that I have made a rehearsall of the birds, and fethered Fowles, which participate most of aire, I will give you a description of the beasts, and shew you, what beasts are bred in those parts, and what my experience hath gathered, by observation of their kinde, and nature, I begin with the most usefull and most beneficiall beast, which is bredd in those parts, which is the Deare.

There are in this Country, three kindes of Deares of which there are greate plenty, and those are very usefull.

Deare of 3. kinds.

First, therefore I will speake of the Elke, which the Salvages call a Mose: it is a very large Deare, with a very faire head, and a broade palme, like the palme of a fallow Deares horne, but much bigger, and is 6. footewide betweene the tipps, which grow curbing downwards: Hee is of the bignesse of a great horse.

Mose or red deare.

There have bin of them, seene that has bin 18. handfulls highe: hee hath a bunch of haire under his jawes: hee is not swifte, but stronge and large in body, and longe legged; in somuch that hee doth use to kneele, when hee feedeth on grasse.

Mose or deare greater than a horse, the height of them 18. hand fulles.

Hee bringeth forth three faunes, or younge ones, at a time; and being made tame, would be good for draught, and more usefull (by reason of their strength) then the Elke of Raushea. These are found very frequent, in the northerne parts of New England, their flesh is very good foode, and much better then our redd Deare of England.

They bringe forth three faunes at one time.

Their hids are by the Salvages converted into very good lether, and dressed as white as milke.

They make good lether of the hides of Deare.

Of this lether, the Salvages make the best shooes, and use to barter away the skinnes to other Salvages, that have none of that kinde of bests in the parts where they live. Very good buffe may be made of the hids, I have seene a hide as large as any horse hide that can be found. There is such abundance of them that the Salvages, at hunting time, have killed of them so many, that they have bestowed six or seaven at a time, upon one English man whome they have borne affection to.

There is a second sort of Deare (lesse then the redd Deare of England, but much bigger then the English fallow Deare) swift of foote, but of a more darke coloure; with some griseld heares. When his coate is full growne in the summer season, his hornes grow curving, with a croked beame, resembling our redd Deare, not with a palme like the fallow Deare.

The midling Deare or fallow Deare.

These bringe 3. fawnes at a time, spotted like our fallow Deares fawnes; the Salvages say, foure, I speake of what I know to be true; for I have killed, in February a doe with three fawnes in her belly, all heared, and ready to fall; for these Deare fall their fawnes, 2. moneths sooner; then the fallow Deare of England. There is such abundance of them, that an hundred have bin found at the spring of the yeare, within the compasse of a mile.

Trappes to catch the Deare. The Salvages take these in trappes made, of their naturall Hempe, which they place in the earth; where they fell a tree for browse, and when hee rounds the tree for the browse, if hee tread on the trapp, hee is horsed up by the legg, by meanes of a pole that starts up and catcheth him.

Their hides the Saluages use for cloathing, and will give for one hide killed in season 2. 3. or 4. beaver skinnes, which will yeild pounds a peece in that Country: so much is the Deares hide prised with them above the beaver. I have made good merchandize of these, the flesh is farre sweeter then the venison of England: and hee feedeth fatt and leane together as a swine, or mutton, where as our Deare of England feede fatt on the out side, they doe not croake at rutting time, nor spendle shafte, nor is their flesh discoloured at rutting. Hee that will impale ground fitting, may be brought once in the yeare, wherewith bats and men hee may take so many to put into that parke, as the hides will pay the chardge of impaleinge, If all these things be well considered, the Deare, as well as the Mose, may have a principall place in the catalogue of commodities.

I for my part may be bould to tell you, that my howse, was not without the flesh of this sort of Deare winter nor summer, the humbles was ever my dogges fee, which by the wesell, was hanged on the barre in the chimney, for his diet only: for hee has brought to my stand a brace in a morning, one after the other before sunne rising, which I have killed. *The Humbles was the doggs fee.*

Roe bucks or Rayne Deare. There is likewise a third sorte of deare, lesse then the other, (which are a kinde of rayne deare) to the southward of all the English plantations, they are excellent good flesh. And these also bring three fawnes at a time, and in this particular the Deare of those parts, excell all the knowne Deare of the whole world.

Wolfes pray upon Deare. On all these the Wolfes doe pray continually the best meanes they have (to escape the wolfes is by swimming to Islands, or necks of land, whereby they escape: for the wolfe will not presume to follow them, untill they see them over a river; then being landed, (they wayting on the shore) undertake the water, and so follow with fresh suite.

Beaver. The next in mine opinion fit to be spoken of, is the Beaver; which is a Beast ordained, for land and water both, and hath fore feete like a cunny, her hinder feete like a goese, mouthed like a cunny, but short eared like a Serat, fishe in summer, and wood in winter, which hee conveyes to his howse built on the water, wherein hee sitts with his tayle hanging in the water, which else would over heate and rot off.

The Beavers cut downe trees, with his fore teeth.

Hee cuts the bodies of trees downe with the fore-teeth, which are so long as a boares tuskes, & with the help of other beavers (which held by each others tayles like a teeme of horses) the hind most with the legg on his shoulder stayed by one of his fore feete against his head) they draw the logg to the habitation appoynted, placing the loggs in a square, and so by pyling one uppon another, they build up a howse, which with boghes is covered very strongly, and placed in some pond to which they make a damme of brush wood like a hedge: so stronge, that I have gone on the top of it crosse the current of that pond. The flesh of this beast is excellent foode. The fleece is a very choise furre, which (before the Salvages had commerce with Christians) they burned of the tayle, this beast is of a masculine vertue for the advancement of Priapus: and is preserved for a dish for the Sachems, or Sagamores: who are the princes of the people but not Kings (as is fondly supposed.)

Beavers at 10. shil. a pound.

The skinnes are the best marchantable commodity, that can be found, to cause ready money to be brought into the land, now that they are raised to 10. shillings a pound.

In five yeares one man gott together 1000. p. in good gold.

A servant of mine in 5. yeares, was thought to have a 1000. p. in ready gold gotten by beaver when hee dyed; whatsoever became of it. And this beast may challenge preheminence in the Catalogue.

The Otter in winter hath a furre as black as Iett.

The Otter of those parts, in winter season, hath a furre so black as jett, and is a furre of very highe price: a good black skinne is worth 3. or 4. Angels of gold. The Flesh is eaten by the Salvages: but how good it is I cannot shew, because it is not eaten by our Nation. Yet is this a beast, that ought to be placed in the number amongst the Commodities of the Country.

The Luseran as bigg as a hound.

The Luseran, or Luseret, is a beast like a Catt: but so bigg as a great hound: with a tayle shorter then a Catt. His clawes are like a Catts, Hee will make a pray of the Deare. His Flesh is dainty meat, like a lambe: his hide is a choise furre, and accompted a good commodity.

The Martin is about the bignesse of a Fox.

The Martin is a beast about the bignes, of a Foxe. His furre is chestnutt coloure, and of those there are greate store in the Northerne parts of the Country, and is a good commodity.

Racowne. The Racowne is a beast as bigg, full out, as a Foxe, with a Bushtayle. His Flesh excellent foode: his oyle precious for the Syattica, his furre course, but the skinnes serve the Salvages for coats: and is with those people of more esteeme, then a coate of beaver, because of the tayles that (hanging round in their order) doe adorne the garment, and is therefore so much esteemed of them. His forefeete are like the feete of an ape; and by the print thereof, in the time of snow, he is followed to his hole, which is commonly in a hollow tree, from whence hee is fiered out, and so taken.

The Foxes red and gray. The Foxes are of two coloures: the one redd, the other gray, these feede on fish; and are good furre, they doe not stinke, as the Foxes of England, but their condition for their pray, is as the Foxes of England.

The Wolfes of diverse coloures. The Wolfes are of divers coloures: some sandy coloured: some griselled, and some black, their foode is fish which they catch, when they passe up the rivers, into the ponds to spawne, at the spring time. The Deare are also their pray, and at summer, when they have whelpes, the bitch will fetch a puppy dogg from our dores, to feede their whelpes with. They are fearefull Curres, and will runne away from a man (that meeteth them by chaunce at a banke end) as fast as any ferefull dogge. These pray upon the Deare very much. The skinnes are used by the Salvages, especially the skinne of the black wolfe, which is esteemed a present for a prince there.

The skin of a black wolfe a present for a prince. When there ariseth any difference betweene prince, and prince, the prince that desires to be reconciled to his neighbouring prince does endeavour to purchase it, by sending him a black wolfes skinne for a present, and the acceptance of such a present is an assurance of reconciliation betweene them; and the Salvages will willingly give 40. beaver skinnes for the purchase of one of these black Wolfes skinnes: and allthough the beast himself be a discommodity, which other Countries of Christendome are subject unto, yet is the skinne of the black wolfe worthy, the title of a commodity, in that respect that hath bin declared.

The Beares afraid of a man. If I should not speake something of the beare, I might happily leave a scruple, in the mindes of some effeminate persone who conceaved of more dainger in them, then there is cause. Therefore to incourage them against all Feare, and Fortifie their mindes against needles danger, I will relate what experience hath taught mee; concerning them, they are beasts that doe no harme in those parts: they feede upon Hurtleburies, Nuts, and Fish, especially shell-fish.

The Beare is a tyrant at a Lobster, and at low water will downe to the Rocks, and groape after them with great diligence.

The Salvages seeing a beare chase him like a dogg and kill him.

Hee will runne away from a man as fast as a litle dogge, If a couple of Salvages chaunce to espie him at his banquet, his running away, will not serve his turne, for they will coate him, and chase him betweene them home to theire howses, where they kill him, to save a laboure in carrying him farre. His Flesh is esteemed venison, and of a better taste then beefe.

His hide is used by the Salvages, for garments, and is more commodious then discommodious, as may passe (with some allowance) with the rest.

Muskewashe.

The Muskewashe, is a beast that frequenteth the ponds. What hee eats I cannot finde. Hee is but a small beast, lesse then a Cunny, and is indeede in those parts no other then a water Ratte, for I have seene the suckers of them digged out of a banke; and at that age, they neither differed in shape coloure, nor size, from one of our greate Ratts. When hee is ould, hee is of the Beavers coloure; and hath passed in waite with our Chapmen for Beaver.

The Male of them have stones, which the Salvages in un caseing of them, leave to the skinne, which is a most delicate perfume, and may compare with any perfume that I know for goodnesse; Then may not this be excluded the Catalogue.

Porcupines.

This Country, in the North parts thereof, hath many Porcupines, but I doe not finde, the beast any way usefull or hurtfull.

Hedghoggs.

There are in those Northerne parts many Hedgehoggs, of the like nature, to our English Hedghoggs.

Conyes of severall sorts.

Here are greate store of Conyes in those parts, of divers coloures; some white, some black, and some gray. Those towards the Southerne parts are very small, but those to the North are as big as the English Cony: their eares are very short. For meate the small rabbit is as good as any that I have eaten of else where.

Squirils of three sorts.

There are Squirils of three sorts, very different in shape and condition; and is gray, and hee is as bigg as the lesser Cony, and keepeth the woods feeding, upon nutts.

Another is red, and hee haunts our howses, and will rob us of our Corne, but the Catt many times, payes him the price of his presumption.

A Flying Squirrill. The third is a little flying Squirill, with bat like winges, which hee spreads when hee jumpes from tree to tree, and does no harme.

Snakes. Now because I am upon a treaty of the beasts, I will place this creature the snake amongst the beasts, having my warrant from the holy Bible; who (though his posture in his passage be so different from all other, being of a more subtile and aidry nature, that hee can make his way without feete, and lifte himselfe above the superficies of the earth, as hee glids along.)

Yet may hee not bee ranked with any, but the beasts, notwithstanding hee frequents the water, as well as the land.

There are of Snakes divers, and of severall kindes, as be with us in England, but that Country hath not so many, as in England have bin knowne.

The generall Salvage name of them is Ascowke.

The rattle Snakes. There is one creeping beast or longe creeple (as the name is in Devonshire,) that hath a rattle at his tayle, that does discover his age; for so many yeares as hee hath lived, so many joynts are in that rattle, which soundeth (when it is in motion,) like pease in a bladder, and this beast is called a rattle Snake; but the Salvages give him the name of Sesick; which some take to be the Adder; and it may well be so; for the Salvages are significiant in their denomination of any thing) and is no lesse hurtfull than the Adder of England, nor no more. I have had my dogge venomed with troubling one of these; and so swelled, that I had thought it would have bin his death: but with one Saucer of Salet oyle powred downe his throat, he has recovered, and the swelling asswaged by the next day. The like experiment hath bin made upon a boy that hath by chaunce troad upon one of these, and the boy never the worse. Therefore it is simplicity in any one that shall tell a bugbeare tale of horrible, or terrible Serpents that are in that land.

Mise. Mise there are good store, and my Lady Woodbees black gray malkin may have pastime enough there: but for Rats, the Country by Nature is troubled with none.

Lyons alwaies in hot Clymats, not in cold. Lyons there are none in New England: it is contrary to the Nature of the beast, to frequent places accustomed to snow; being like the Catt, that will hazard the burning of her tayle rather than abide from the fire.

Chap. VI.

Of Stones and Minerals.

NOw (for as much as I have in a breife abstract shewed you the Creatures: whose specificall Natures doe simpathise with the elements of fire and aire) I will come to speake of the Creatures that participate of earth more then the other two, which is stones.

Marble. And first of the Marble for building; whereof there is much in those parts, in so much there is one bay in the land, that beareth the name of Marble harber, because of the plenty of Marble there: and these are usefull for building of Sumpteous Pallaces.

Limestone. And because, no good building can be made permanent, or durable, without Lime: I will let you understand that there is good Limestone neere to the river of Monatoquinte at uttaquatockto my knowledge and we hope other places too, (that I have not taken so much notice of) may have the like, or better: and those stones are very convenient for building.

Chalk. Chalke stones there are neere Squantos Chappell shewed me by a Salvage.

Slate. There is abundance of excellent Slate in divers places of the Country: and the best that ever I beheld for covering of howses: and the inhabitants have made good use of these materials for building.

Whetstones. There is a very usefull Stone in the Land, and as yet there is found out but one place where they may be had, in the whole Country, Ould Woodman, (that was choaked at Plimmouth after hee had played the unhappy Markes man when hee was pursued by a carelesse fellow that was new come into the Land) they say laboured to get a patent of it to himselfe. Hee was beloved of many, and had many sonnes, that had a minde to engrosse that commodity. And I cannot spie any mention made of it in the woodden prospect.

Therefore I begin to suspect his aime; that it was for himselfe, and therefore will I not discover it, it is the Stone so much commended by *Ovid,* because love delighteth to make his habitation in a building of those materials, where hee advises. Those that seeke for love to doe it, *Duris in Cotibus illum.*

This stone the Salvages doe call *Cos,* and of these (on the

North end of Richmond Island) are store, and those are very excellent good for edg'd tooles: I envy not his happinesse. I have bin there: viewed the place, liked the commodity: but will not plant so Northerly for that, nor any other commodity that is there to be had.

Loadstones. There are Loadstones also in the Northerne parts of the land: and those which were found are very good, and are a commodity worth the noteing.

Ironstones. Iron stones there are abundance: and severall sorts of them knowne.

Lead. Lead ore is there likewise, and hath bin found by the breaking of the earth, which Frost hath made mellow.

Black Lead. Black Leade I have likewise found very good, which the Salvages use to paint their faces with.

Read Lead. Red Leade is there likewise in great abundance.

Boll. There is very excellent Boll Armoniack.

Vermilion. There is most excellent Vermilion. All these things the Salvages make some litle use of, and doe finde them on the circumference of the Earth.

Brimstone. Brimstone mines there are likewise.

Tinne. Mines of Tinne, are likewise knowne to be in those parts: which will in short time be made use of: and this cannot be accompted a meane commodity.

Copper. Copper mines are there found likewise: that will enrich the Inhabitants. But untill theire younge Cattell, be growne hardy labourers in the yoake, that the Plough and the Wheate may be seene more plentifully, it is a worke must be forborne.

Silver. They say there is a Silver, and a gold mine found by Captaine Littleworth: if hee get a patent of it to himselfe, hee will surely change his name.

Chap. VII.

Of the Fishes, and what commodity they proove.

AMong Fishes First I will begin with the Codd, because it is the most commodious of all fish, as may appeare, by the use which is made of them in foraigne parts.

Codd. The Codd fishing is much used in America, (whereof New England is a part) in so much as 300. Sayle of shipps, from divers parts, have used to be im ployed yearely in that trade,

I have seene in one Harboure, next Richmond Island 15. Sayle of shipps at one time, that have taken in them, driyed Codds for Spaine, and the Straights (and it has bin found that the Saylers have made 15. 18. 20. 22. p. share for a common man. *15. Shipps at one time for Codd.*

The Coast aboundeth with such multitudes of Codd, that the inhabitants of New England doe dunge their grounds with Codd; and it is a commodity better than the golden mines of the Spanish Indies; for without dried Codd the Spaniard, Portingal and Italian, would not be able to vittell of a shipp for the Sea; and I am sure at the Canaries it is the principall commodity: which place lyeth neere New England very convenient, for the vending of this commodity, one hundred of these being at the price of 300. of New found land Codds, greate store of traine oyle, is mayd of the livers of the Codd, and is a commodity that without question will enrich the inhabitants of New England quickly; and is therefore a principall commodity. *Oyle mayd of the livers of the Codd.*

The Basse is an excellent Fish, both fresh and Salte one hundred whereof salted (at a market) have yielded 5. p. They are so large, the head of one will give a good eater a dinner, and for daintinesse of diet, they excell the Marybones of Beefe. There are such multitudes, that I have seene stopped into the river close adjoyning to my howse with a sand at one tide, so many as will loade a ship of a 100. Tonnes. *A 100 Basse sould for 5. p.*

Other places have greater quantities in so much, as wagers have bin layed, that one should not throw a stone in the water, but that hee should hit a fish.

I my selfe, at the turning of the tyde, have seene such multitudes passe out of a pound, that it seemed to mee, that one might goe over their backs drishod.

These follow the bayte up the rivers, and sometimes are followed for bayte and chased into the bayes, and shallow waters, by the grand pise: and these may have also a prime place in the Catalogue of Commodities.

The Mackarels are the baite for the Basse, and these have bin chased into the shallow waters, where so many thousands have shott themselves a shore with the surfe of the Sea, that whole hogges-heads have bin taken up on the Sands; and for length they excell any of other parts: they have bin measured 18. and 19. inches in length and seaven in breadth: and are taken with a drayle, (as boats use to passe to and froe at Sea on businesse) in very greate quantities all along the Coaste. *Mackarell are baite for Basse.*

The Fish is good, salted; for store against the winter, as well as fresh, and to be accounted a good Commodity.

Sturgeon. This Sturgeon in England is *regalis piscis.* every man in New England may catch what he will, there are multitudes of them, and they are much fatter then those that are brought into England from other parts, in so much as by reason of their fatnesse, they doe not looke white, but yellow, which made a Cooke presume they were not so good as them of Roushea: silly fellow that could not understand that it is the nature of fish salted, or pickelled, the fatter the yellower being best to preserve.

For the taste I have warrant of Ladies of worth, with choise pallats for the commendations, who liked the taste so well, that they esteemed it beyond the Sturgeon of other parts, and sayd they were deceaved in the lookes: therefore let the Sturgeon passe for a Commodity.

Salmon. Of Salmons there is greate abundance: and these may be allowed for a Commodity, and placed in the Catallogue.

Herrings. Of Herrings, there is greate store, fat, and faire: and (to my minde) as good as any I have seene, and these may be preserved, and made a good commodity at the Canaries.

Great plenty of Eeles. Of Eeles there is abundance, both in the Saltwaters, and in the fresh: and the fresh water Eele there (if I may take the judgement of a London Fishmonger) is the best that hee hath found in his life time. I have with jieele potts found my howse hold, (being nine persons, besides doggs) with them, taking them every tide, (for 4. moneths space,) and preserving of them for winter store: and these may proove a good commodity.

Smelts. Of Smelts there is such abundance, that the Salvages doe take them up the rivers with baskets, like sives.

Shadds or Allizes taken to dunge ground. There is a Fish, (by some called shadds, by some allizes) that at the spring of the yeare, passe up the rivers to spaune in the ponds; and are taken in such multitudes in every river, that hath a pond at the end, that the Inhabitants doung their ground with them. You may see in one towneship a hundred acres together, set with these Fish, every acre taking 1000. of them: and an acre thus dressed will produce and yeald so much corne as 3. acres without fish: and (least any Virginea man would inferre hereupon, that the ground of New England is barren, because they use no fish in setting their corne, I desire them to be remembred, the cause is plaine in Virginea) they have it not to sett. But this practise is onely for the Indian Maize (which must be set by hands) not for English graine: and this is therefore a commodity there.

Turbut or Hallibut. There is a large sized fish called Hallibut, or Turbut: some are taken so bigg that two men have much a doe to hale them into the boate; but there is such plenty, that the fisher men onely eate the heads, and finnes, and throw away the bodies: such in Paris would yeeld 5. or 6. crownes a peece: and this is no discommodity.

Plaice. There are excellent Plaice and easily taken. They (at flowing water) do almost come ashore, so that one may stepp but halfe a foote deepe, and prick them up on the sands: and this may passe with some allowance.

Hakes. Hake is a dainty white fish, and excellent vittell fresh; and may passe with other commodities, because there are multitudes.

Pilchers. There are greate store of Pilchers: at Michelmas, in many places, I have seene the Cormorants in length 3. miles feedinge upon the Sent.

Lobsters. Lobsters are there infinite in store in all the parts of the land, and very excellent. The most use that I made of them, in 5. yeares after I came there was but to baite my Hooke for to catch Basse, I had bin so cloyed with them the first day I went a shore.

This being knowne, they shall passe for a commodity to the inhabitants; for the Salvages will meete 500, or 1000. at a place where Lobsters come in with the tyde, to eate, and save dried for store, abiding in that place, feasting and sporting a moneth or 6. weekes together.

Oysters. There are greate store of Oysters in the entrance of all Rivers: they are not round as those of England, but excellent fat, and all good. I have seene an Oyster banke a mile at length.

Mustles. Mustles there are infinite store, I have often gon to Wassaguscus; where were excellent Mustles to eate (for variety) the fish is so fat and large.

Clames. Clames is a shellfish, which I have seene sold in Westminister for 12. pe. the skore. These our swine feede upon; and of them there is no want, every shore is full, it makes the swine proove exceedingly, they will not faile at low water to be with them. The Salvages are much taken with the delight of this fishe; and are not cloyed (notwithstanding the plenty) for our swine we finde it a good commodity.

Raser fish. Raser fishes there are.

Freele. Freeles there are, Cockles, and Scallopes, and divers other sorts of Shellfishe, very good foode.

Now that I have shewed you what commodities are there to be had in the Sea, for a Market; I will shew what is in the Land also, for the comfort of the inhabitants, wherein it doth abound. And because my taske is an abstract, I will discover to them the commodity thereof.

Fresh fish, Trouts, Carpes, Breames, Pikes, Roches, Perches, Tenches, and Eeles. There are in the rivers, and ponds, very excellent Trouts, Carpes, Breames, Pikes, Roches, Perches, Tenches, Eeles, and other fishes, such as England doth afford, and as good, for variety; yea many of them much better; and the Natives of the inland parts, doe buy hookes of us, to catch them with, and I have knowne the time, that a Trouts hooke hath yeelded a beaver skinne, which hath bin a good commodity to those that have bartered them away.

These things I offer to your consideration (curteous Reader) and require you to shew mee the like in any part of the knowne world if you can.

Chap. VIII.

Of the goodnes of the Country and the Waters.

Foode, and Fire. NOw since it is a Country so infinitely blest with foode, and fire, to roast or boyle our Flesh and Fish, why should any man feare for cold there, in a Country warmer in the winter, than some parts of France and neerer the Sunne: unles hee be one of those that Salomon bids goe to the Ant and the Bee.

Noe Boggs. There is no boggy ground, knowne in all the Country, from whence the Sunne may exhale unwholsom vapors: But there are divers arematicall herbes, and plants, as Sassafras, Muske, Roses, Violets, Balme, Lawrell, Hunnisuckles, and the like, that with their vapors perfume the aire; and it has bin a thing much observed that, shipps have come from Virginea where there have bin scarce five men able to hale a rope, untill they have come within 40. Degrees of latitude, and smell the sweet aire of the shore, where they have suddainly recovered. *Perfumed aire with sweet herbes.*

Of Waters. And for the water, therein excelleth Canaan by much; for the Land is so apt for Fountaines, a man cannot digg amisse, therefore if the Abrahams and Lots of our times come thether, there needs be no contention for wells.

Besides there are waters of most excellent vertues, worthy admiration.

At Ma-re-Mount, there was a water (by mee discovered) that is most excellent for the cure of Melancolly probatum.

The Cure of mellancolly at Ma-remount.

At weenasemute is a water, the vertue whereof is, to cure barrennesse. The place taketh his name of that Fountaine which signifieth quick spring, or quickning spring probatum.

The cure of Barrennesse.

Neere Squantos Chappell (a place so by us called) is a Fountaine, that causeth a dead sleepe for 48. howres, to those that drinke 24. ounces at a draught, and so proportionably. The Salvages that are Powahs at set times use it, and reveale strang things to the vulgar people by meanes of it, So that in the delicacy of waters, and the conveniency of them, Canaan came not neere this Country.

Water procuring a dead sleepe.

New England excels Canaan in fountaines.

As for the Milke and Hony which that Canaan flowed with, it is supplyed by the plenty of birds; beasts and Fish, whereof Canaan could not boast her selfe.

Milke and Hony supplied.

Yet never the lesse (since the Milke came by the industry of the first Inhabitants,) let the cattell be cherished that are at this time in New England, and forborne but a litle, I will aske no long time; no more, but untill the Brethren have converted one Salvage, and made him a good Christian, and I may be bold to say, Butter and cheese will be cheaper there, then ever it was in Canaan. It is cheaper there then in old England at this present, for there are store of Cowes; considering the people: which (as my intelligence gives) is 12000. persons, and in gods name let the people have their desire, who writes to their freinds, to come out of Sodome, to the land of Canaan, a land that flowes with Milke and Hony.

A plain paralell to Canaan.

And I appeale to any man of judgement whether it be not a Land, that for her excellent indowments of Nature may passe for a plaine paralell to Canaan of Israell, being in a more temporat Climat, this being in 40. Degrees and that in 30.

The Request for the Nomination of New Canaan.

Chap. IX.

A Perspective to view the Country by.

AS for the Soyle, I may be bould to commend the fertility thereof, and preferre it before the Soyle of England, (our Native Country) and I neede not to produce more then one argument for proffe thereof, because it is so infallible.

The Soyle.

The grouth of Hempe.

Hempe is a thing by Husband men in generall ageed upon, to prosper best, in the most fertile Soyle: and experience hath taught this rule, that Hempe seede prospers so well in New England, that it shewteth up to be tenne foote high and tenne foote and a halfe, which is twice so high as the ground in old England produce it, which argues New England the more fertile of the two.

The aire.

As for the aire, I will produce but one proffe for the maintenance of the excellency thereof; which is so generall, as I assure myselfe it will suffice.

No cold Cough or murre.

No man living there; was ever knowne to be troubled with a cold, a cough, or a murre, but many men comming sick out of Virginea to New Canaan, have instantly recovered with the helpe of the purity of that aire; no man ever surfeited himselfe either by eating or drinking.

The plenty of the Land.

As for the plenty of that Land, it is well knowne that no part of Asia, Affrica, or Europe; affordeth deare that doe bring forth any more then one single faune; and in New Canaan the Deare are accustomed to bring forth 2. and 3. faunes at a time.

Besides there are such infinite flocks of Fowle, and Multitudes of fish both in the fresh waters, and also on the Coast, that the like hath not else where bin discovered by any traveller.

Windes.

The windes there are not so violent as in England; which is prooved by the trees that grow in the face of the winde by the Sea Coast, for there they doe not lean from the winde as they doe in England, as we have heard before.

Raine.

The Raine is there more moderate then in England, which thing I have noted in all the time of my residence to be so.

The Coast.

The Coast is low Land, and not high Land: and hee is of a weake capacity that conceaveth otherwise of it, because it cannot be denied, but that boats may come a ground in all places along the Coast, and especially within the Compas of the Massachusets patent, where the prospect is fixed.

The Harboures are not to be bettered, for safety, and goodnesse of ground, for ancorage, and (which is worthy observation ;) shipping will not there be furred, neither are they subject to wormes, as in Virginea, and other places. *Harboures.*

Let the Scituation also of the Country be considered (together with the rest, which is discovered in the front of this abstract,) and then I hope no man will hold this land unworthy to be intituled by the name of the second Canaan. *Scituation.*

And since the Seperatists, are desirous to have the denomination thereof, I am become an humble Suter on their behalfe for your consents (courteous Readers) to it, before I doe shew you what Revels they have kept in New Canaan. *The Nomination.*

CHAP. X.

Of the Great Lake of Erocoise in New England, and the commodities thereof.

WEstwards from the Massachussets bay (which lyeth in 42. Degrees and 30. Minutes of Northern latitude) is scituated a very spacious Lake (called of the Natives the Lake of Erocoise) which is farre more excellent then the Lake of Genezereth in the Country of Palestina, both in respect of the greatnes and properties thereof; and likewise of the manifould commodities it yealdeth: the circumference of which Lake is reputed to be 240. miles at the least: and it is distant from the Massachussets bay 300. miles, or there abouts: wherein are very many faire Islands, where innumerable flocks of severall sorts of Fowle doe breede, Swannes, Geese, Ducks, Widgines, Teales, and other water Fowle. *Fowle innumerable.*

There are also more abundance of Beavers, Deare, and Turkies breed about the part of that lake, then in any place in all the Country of New England; and also such multitudes of fish, (which is a great part of the foode, that the Beavers live upon,) that it is a thing to be admired at: So that about this Lake, is the principallst place for a plantation in all New Canaan, both for pleasure and proffit. *Multitudes of Fish.* *The prime place of New Canaan.*

Here may very many brave Townes and Citties be erected which may have intercourse one with another by water, very commodiously: and it is of many men of good judgement, accounted the prime seate for the Metropolis of New Canaan, From this Lake Northwards is derived the famous River of Canada, (so named of Monsier de Cane a French Lord, that first planted a Colony of French in America, there called Nova Francia, from whence Captaine Kerke of late, by taking that plantation, brought home in one shipp (as a Seaman of his Company, reported in my hearing) 25000. Beaver skinnes.

So named of Monsier de Cane.

And from this Lake Southwards, trends that goodly River called of the Natives Patomack, which dischardgeth herselfe in the parts of Virginea, from whence it is navigable by shipping of great Burthen up to the Falls (which lieth in 41. Degrees, and a halfe of North latitude:) and from the Lake downe to the Falls by a faire current. This River is navigable for vessels of good Burthen; and thus much hath often bin related by the Natives, and is of late found to be certaine.

Patomack.

They have also made description of great heards of well growne beasts, that live about the parts of this Lake, such as the Christian world (untill this discovery) hath not bin acquainted with. These beasts are of the bignesse of a Cowe, their Flesh being very good foode, their hides good lether, their fleeces very usefull, being a kinde of wolle, as fine almost as the wolle of the Beaver, and the Salvages doe make garments thereof.

Great heards of Beasts as bigg as Cowes.

It is tenne yeares since first the relation of these things came to the eares of the English: at which time wee were but slender proficients in the language of the Natives, and they, (which now have attained to more perfection of English, could not then make us rightly apprehend their meaninge.

Wee supposed, when they spake of Beasts thereabouts as high as men, they have made report of men all over hairy like Beavers, in so much as we questioned them, whether they eate of the Beavers, to which they replyed Matta, (noe) saying they were almost Beavers Brothers. This relation at that time wee concluded to be fruitles, which since, time hath made more apparent.

About the parts of this Lake may be made a very greate Commodity by the trade of furres, to inrich those that shall plant there; a more compleat discovery of those parts: is (to my knowleadge) undertaken by Henry Ioseline Esquier sonne of Sir Thomas Ioseline of Kent Knight, by the approbation and appointement of that Heroick and very good Common wealths man Captaine Iohn Mason Esquier, a true foster Father and lover of vertue, (who at his owne chardge) hath fitted Master Ioseline and imployed him to that purpose, who no doubt will performe as much as is expected, if the Dutch (by gettinge into those parts before him, doe not frustrate his so hopefull and laudable designes.

Henry Ieseline employed for discovery.

It is well knowne, they aime at that place, and have a possibility to attaine unto the end of their desires therein, by meanes, if the River of Mohegan, which of the English is named Hudsons River (where the Dutch have setled: to well fortified plantations already. If that River be derived from the Lake as our Country man in his prospect affirmes it to be, and if they get and fortifie this place also, they will gleane away the best of the Beaver both from the French and the English, who have hitherto lived wholely by it, and very many old planters have gained good estates out of small beginnings by meanes thereof.

And it is well knowne to some of our Nation that have lived in the Dutch plantation: that the Dutch have gained by Beaver 20000. pound a yeare.

The Dutch have a great trade of Beaver in Hudsons River.

The Salvages make report of 3. great Rivers that issue out of this Lake 2. of which are to us knowne, the one to be Patomack, the other Canada, and why may not the third be found there likewise, which they describe to trend westward, which is conceaved to discharge herselfe into the South Sea. The Salvages affirme that they have seene shipps in this Lake with 4. Masts which have taken from thence for their ladinge earth, that is conjectured to be some minerall stuffe.

There is probability enough for this, and it may well be thought, that so great a confluxe of waters as are there gathered together, must be vented by some great Rivers: and that if the third River (which they have made mention of) proove to be true as the other two have done: there is no doubt but that the passage to the East India, may be obtained, without any such daingerous and fruitlesse inquest by the Norwest, as hetherto hath bin endeavoured: And there is no Traveller of any resonable capacity, but will graunt, that about this Lake must be innumerable springes, and by that meanes many fruitfull, and pleasant pastures all about it, It hath bin observed that the inland part (witnes Neepnet) are more pleasant and fertile then the borders of the Sea coaste. And the Country about Erocoise is (not without good cause) compared to Delta the most fertile parte

Passage to the East Indies.

The Country of Erocois as fertile

as Delta in Ægypt. in all Ægypt, that aboundeth with Rivers and Rivalets derived from Nilus fruitfull channell, like vaines from the liver, so in each respect is this famous Lake of Erocoise.

Ad therefore it would be adjudged an irreparable oversight to protract time, and suffer the Dutch (who are but intruders upon his Majesties most hopefull Country of New England) to possesse themselves of that so plesant and commodious Country of Erocoise before us: being (as appeareth) the principall part of all New Canaan for plantation, and not elsewhere to be paralelld in all the knowne world.

NEW CANAANS GENIVS

EPILOGVS.

THou that art by Fates degree,
Or Providence ordain'd to see,
Natures wonder, her rich store,
Ne'-r discovered before,
Th' admired Lake of Erocoise,
And fertile Borders now rejoyce,
See what multitudes of Fish,
Shee presents to fitt thy dish,
If rich furres thou dost adore,
And of Beaver Fleeces store,
See the Lake where they abound,
And what pleasures els are found,
There chast Leda free from fire,
Does enjoy her hearts desire,
Mongst the flowry bancks at ease,
Live the sporting Najades,
Bigglim'd Druides whose browes,
Bewtified with greenebowes,
See the Nimphes how they doe make,
Fine Meanders from the Lake,
Twining in and out as they,
Through the pleasant groves make way,
Weaving by the shady trees,
Curious Anastomases,
Where the harmeles Turtles breede,
And such usefull Beasts doe feede,
As no Traveller can tell,
Els where how to paralell,
Colcos golden Fleece reject,
This deserveth best respect,
In sweete Peans let thy voyce,
Sing the praise of Erocoise,
Peans to advance her name,
New Canaans everlasting fame.

NEW ENGLISH CANAAN,

OR NEW CANAAN.

The Third Booke.

Containing a description of the People that are planted there, what remarkable Accidents have happened there, since they were setled, what Tenants they hould, together with the practise of their Church.

CHAP. I.

Of a great League made with the Plimmouth Planters after their arrivall, by the Sachem of those Territories.

THe Sachem of the Territories, where the Planters of New England are setled, that are the first of the now Inhabitants of New Canaan, not knowing what they were, or whether they would be freindes or foes, and being desirous to purchase their freindship, that hee might have the better Assurance of quiet tradinge with them (which hee conceived would be very advantagious to him) was desirous to prepare an Ambassador, with commission to treat on his behalfe, to that purpose; and having one that had beene in England taken by) a worthlesse man) out of other partes, and after left there by accident, this Salvage hee instructed, how to be have himselfe, in the treaty of peace, and the more, to give him incouragement to adventure his person, amongst these new come inhabitants, which was a thinge, hee durst not himselfe attempt, without security or hostage, promised that Salvage freedome, who had beene detained there as theire Captive: which offer hee accepted, and accordingly came to the Planters, salutinge them with wellcome, in the English phrase, which was of them admired, to heare a Salvage there speake in their owne language, and used him great courtesie: to whome hee declared the cause of his comminge, and contrived the businesse so, that hee brought the Sachem and the English together, betweene whome was a firme league concluded, which yet continueth. After which league the Sachem being in company with the other whome hee had freed, and suffered to live with the English, espijnge a place where a hole had been made in the grounde, where was their store of powder layed to be preserved from danger of fire (under ground) demanded of the Salvage what the English had hid there under ground, who answered the plague, at which hee starteled, because of the great mortality lately happened, by meanes of the plague, (as it is conceaved) and the Salvage the more to encrease his feare told the Sachem if he should give offence to the English party, they would let out the plague to destroy thĕ all, which kept him in great awe. Not longe after being at varience with another Sachem borderinge upon his Territories, he came in solemne manner and intreated the Governour, that he would let out the plague to destroy the Sachem, and his men who were his enemies, promising that he himselfe, and all his posterity would be their everlasting freindes, so great an opinion he had of the English.

A Salvage sent an Ambassador to the English at their first comminge.

The Sachem feared the Plague.

CHAP. II.

Of the entertainment of Mr. Westons people sent to settle a plantation there.

MAster Thomas weston a Merchant of London that had been at some cost, to further the Brethren of new Plimmouth, in their designes for these partes, shipped a company of Servants, fitted with provition of all sorts; for the undertaking of a Plantation to be setled there, with an intent to follow after them in parson. These servants at first arived at new Plimmouth where they were entertained with court holy bread, by the Brethren, they were made very wellcome, in shew at least: -there these servants goodes were landed, with promises to be assisted in the choise of a convenient place, and still the good cheare went forward, and the strong liquors walked. In the meane time the Brethren were in consultation, what was best for their advantage singing the songe, *Frustra sapit, qui sibi non sapit.*

Court holy bread at Plimmouth.

This plantation would hinder the present practice, and future profit, & Master Weston an able man would want for no supplies, upon the returne of Beaver, and so might be a plantation that might keepe them under, who had a Hope to be the greatest, besides his people were no chosen Seperatists, but men made choice of at all adventures, fit to have served for the furtherance of Master Westons undertakinges: and that was as much as hee neede to care for: ayminge at Beaver principally, for the better effecting of his purpose. Now when the Plimmouth men began to finde, that Master Westons mens store of provition grew short with feasting, then they hasted them to a place called Wessaguscus, in a weake case, and there left them fasting.

Chap. III.

Of a Battle fought at the Massachussets, betweene the English and the French.

THe Planters of Plimmouth, at their last being in those parts, having defaced the monument of the ded at Pasonayessit (by taking away the herse Cloath which was two greate Beares skinnes sowed together at full length, and propped up over the grave of Chuatawbacks mother,) the Sachem of those territories, being inraged at the same, stirred up his men in his bee halfe, to take revenge: and having gathered his men together, hee begins to make an oration in this manner. When last the glorious light of all the skey was underneath this globe, and Birds grew silent, I began to settle as my (custome is) to take repose; before mine eies were fast closed, mee thought I saw a vision, (at

The Sachems Oration.

which my) spirit was much troubled, & trembling at that dolefull sight, a spirit cried aloude (behold my sonne) whom I have cherisht, see the papps that gave thee suck, the hands that lappd thee warme and fed thee oft, canst thou forget to take revenge of those uild people, that hath my monument defaced in despitefull manner, disdaining our ancient antiquities, and honourable Customes: See now the Sachems grave lies like unto the common people, of ignoble race defaced; thy mother doth complaine, implores thy aide against this theevish people, new come hether if this be suffered, I shall not rest in quiet within my everlasting habitation. This said, the spirit vanished, and I all in a sweat, not able scarce to speake, began to gett some strength, and recollect my spirits that were fled, all which I thought to let you understand, to have your Councell, and your aide likewise; this being spoken, straight way arose the grand Captaine, and cried aloud come, let us to Armes, it doth concerne us all, let us bid them Battaile; so to Armes they went, and laid weight for the Plimmouth boate, and forceinge them to forsake their landinge place, they seeke another best for their convenience, thither the Salvages repaire in hope to have the like successe, but all in vaine, for the English Captaine warily foresaw, (and perceavinge their plot) knew the better how to order his men fit for Battaile in that place, hee bouldly leading his men on, rainged about the feild to and fro, and taking his best advantage, lets fly, and makes the Salvages give ground, the English followed them fiercely on and made thĕm take trees for their shelter, (as their custome is) from whence their Captaine let flie a maine, yet no man was hurt, at last lifting up his right arm to draw a fatall shaft (as hee then thought) to end this difference, received a shott upon his elbow,) and straight way fled, by whose example, all the army followed the same way; and yealded up the honor of the day, to the English party; who were such a terror to them after, that the Salvages durst never make to a head against them any more.

A spirit mooving the Sachem to Warre.

The grand Captaine makes a Speech.

The maine Battaile.

The feild wonne by the English.

Chap. IV.

Of a Parliament held at Wessaguscus, and the Actes.

Some lazy people. MAster Westons Plantation beinge setled at Wessaguscus, his Servants, many of them lazy persons, that would use no endeavour to take the benefit of the Country, some of them fell sicke and died.

A lusty fellow. One amongst the rest an able bodied man, that ranged the woodes, to see what it would afford, lighted by accident on an Indian barne, and from thence did take a capp full of corne; the Salvage owner of it, finding by the foote some English had bin there came to the Plantation, and mad complaint after this manner.

The cheife Commander of the Company one this occation called a Parliament of all his people but those that were sicke, and ill at ease. And wisely now they must consult, upon this huge complaint, that a privy knife, or stringe of beades would well enough have qualified, and Edward Iohnson was a spetiall judge of this businesse; the fact was there in repetition, construction made, that it was fellony, and by the Lawes of England punished with death, and this in execution must be put, for an example, and likewise to appease the Salvage, when straight wayes one arose, mooved as it were with some compassion, and said hee could not well gaine say the former sentence, yet hee had conceaved within the compasse of his braine a Embrion, that was of spetiall consequence to be delivered, and cherished hee said, that it would most aptly serve to pacifie the Salvages complaint, and save the life of one that might (if neede should be) stand them in some good steede, being younge and stronge, fit for resistance against an enemy, which might come unexpected for any thinge they knew, The Oration made was liked of every one, and hee intreated to proceede to shew the meanes how this may be performed: sayes hee, you all agree that one must die, and one shall die, this younge mans cloathes we will take of, and put upon one, that is old and impotent, a sickly person that cannot escape death, such is the disease one him confirmed, that die hee must, put the younge mans cloathes on this man, and let the sick person be hanged in the others steede: Amen sayes one, and so sayes many more.

A poore complaint. Edward Iohnson a cheife Iudge Maide a hainous fact.

A fine device.

A wise sentence.

To hange a sick-man in the others steede.

And this had like to have prooved their finall sentence, and being there confirmed by Act of Parliament, to after ages for a President: But that one with a ravenus voyce, begunne to croake and bellow for revenge, and put by that conclusive motion, alledging such deceipts might be a meanes here after to exasperate the mindes of the complaininge Salvages and that by his death, the Salvages should see their zeale to Iustice, and therefore hee should die: this was concluded; yet neverthelesse a scruple was made; now to countermaund this act, did represent itselfe unto their mindes, which was how they should doe to get the mans good wil: this was indeede a spetiall obstacle: for without (that they all agreed) it would be dangerous, for any man to attempt the execution of it, lest mischeife should befall them every man; hee was a person, that in his wrath, did seeme to be a second Sampson, able to beate out their branes with the jawbone of an Asse: therefore they called the man and by perswation got him fast bound in jest, and then hanged him up hard by in good earnest, who with a weapon, and at liberty, would have put all those wise judges of this Parliament to a pitifull *non plus*, (as it hath been credibly reported) and made the cheife Iudge of them all buckell to him.

Very fit Iustice.

A dangerous Attempt.

Jesting turned to earnest.

Chap. V.

Of a Massacre made upon the Salvages at Wessaguscus.

AFter the end of that Parliament, some of the plantation there, about three persons went to live with Checatawback & his company, and had very good quarter, for all the former quarrell, with the Plimmouth planters: they are not like will sommers, to take one for another. There they purposed to stay untill Master Westons arrivall: but the Plimmouth men intendinge no good to him (as appered by the consequence) came in the meane time to Wessaguscus, and there pretended to feast the Salvages of those partes, bringing with them Porke, and thinges for the purpose, which they sett before the Salvages. They eate thereof without suspition of any mischeife, who were taken upon a watchword

Good quarters with the Salvages.

A plott from Plimmouth.

Salvages killed with their one weapons. given, and with their owne knives (hanging about their neckes) were by the Plimmouth planters stabd and slaine: one of which were hanged up there, after the slaughter.

News carried. In the meane time the Sachem had knowledge of this accident, by one that ranne to his Countrymen, at the Massachussets, and gave them intelligence of the newes; after which time the Salvages there consultinge of the matter, in the night (when the other English feareles *A revenge.* of danger were a sleepe,) knockt them all in the head, in revenge of the death of their Countrymen: but if the Plimmouth Planters had really intended good to Master Weston, or those men, why had they not kept the Salvages alive in Custody, untill they had secured the other English? Who by meanes of this evill mannaginge of the businesse lost their lives and the whole plantation was dissolved thereupon, as was likely for feare of a revenge to follow, as a relatione to this cruell antecedent; and when Master Weston came over; hee found thinges at an evill exigent, by means thereof: But could not tell, how it was brought about:

The Salvages of the Massachussets that could not imagine, from whence these men should come, or to what end, seeing them performe such unexpected actions; neither could tell by what name, properly to distinguish them, did from that time afterwards, call the English Planters Wotawquenange, which in their language signifieth stabbers or Cutthroates, *The Salvages call the English cut-throats.* and this name was received by those that came there after for good, being then unacquainted with the signification of it, for many yeares following, untill from a Southerly Indian, that understood English well, I was by demonstration, made to conceave the interpretation of it, and rebucked these other, that it was not forborne: The other callinge us by the name of Wotoquansawge, what that doth signifie, hee said hee was not able by any demonstration to expresse and my neighbours durst no more in my hearinge, call us by the name formerly used, for feare of my displeasure.

Chap. VI.

Of the surprizinge of a Merchants Shipp in Plimmouth harbour.

THis Merchant a man of worth, arrivinge in the parts of New Canaan, and findinge that his Plantation was dissolved, some of his men slaine, some dead with sicknes, and the rest at Plimmouth; hee was perplexed in his minde about the matter, comminge as hee did with supply, and means to have rased their fortunes and his one exceedingly and seeinge what had happened resolved to make some stay in the Plimmouth harbour, and this suted to their purpose, wherefore the Brethren did congratulate with him at his safe arrivall, and their best of entertainement for a swetning cast, deploring the disaster of his Plantation, and glozing upon the text, alledging the mischeivous intent of the Salvages there, which by freindly intelligence of their neighbours, was discovered before it came to be full summed: so that they lost not all, allthough they saved not all: and this they pretended to proceede from the Fountaine of love & zeale to him; and Christianity, and to chastise the insolency of the Salvages, of which that part had some dangerous persons. And this as an article of the new creede of Canaan, would they have received of every new commer there to inhabit; that the Salvages are a dangerous people, subtill, secreat, and mischeivous, and that it is dangerous to live separated, but rather together, and so be under their Lee, that none might trade for Beaver, but their pleasure, as none doe or shall doe there: nay they will not be reduced to any other song yet, of the Salvages to the southward of Plimmouth, because they would have none come there, sayinge that hee that will sit downe there must come stronge: but I have found the Massachussets Indian more full of humanity, then the Christians, & haue had much better quarter with them; yet I observed not their humors, but they mine, although my great number that I landed were dissolved, and my Company as few as might be: for I know that this falls out infallibly where two Nations meete, one must rule, and the other be ruled, before a peace can be hoped for: and for a Christian to submit to the rule of a Salvage you will say, is both shame and dishonor: (at least) it is my opinion, and my practise was accordingly, and I

The Merchant with supply.

A glosse upon the false text.

Where two nations meet one must rule the other must be ruled or no quietnes.

have the better quarter by the meanes thereof. The more Salvages the better quarter, the more Christians the worser quarter I found, as all the indifferent minded Planters can testifie. Now whiles the Merchant was ruminatinge on this mishapp, the Plimmouth Planters perceivinge that hee had furnished himselfe with excellent Commodities, fit for the Merchandise of the Country, (and holding it good to fish in trobled waters, and so get a snatch unseene) practised in secret with some other in the land, whom they thought apt to imbrace the benefit of such a cheat, and it was concluded and resolved upon, that all this shipp and goodes should be confiscated, for businesse done by him, the Lord knowes when, or where a letter must be framed to them, and handes unto it, to be there warrant, this should shadow them; That is the first practise they will insane a man, and then pretend that Iustice must be done: They cause the Merchant (secure) to come a shore, and then take him in hold, shewing they are compelled unto it legally, and enter strait abord peruse the Cargazowne, and then deliver up the Charge of her to their Confederates: and how much lesse this is then Piraty, let any practise in the Admiralty be judge. The Merchant, his shipp and goodes confiscated, himselfe a prisoner, and threatned so to be sent and conveyed to England, there to receave the somme of all that did belonge to him a malefactor (and a great one to) this hee good man, indured with patience, longe time, untill the best of all his goodes were quite dispersed, and every his proportion, the Merchant was inlarged, his shipp a burthen to the owner now, his undertakinges in these partes beinge quite overthrowne, was redelivered, and bondes of him were taken not to prosecute, hee being greived hereat, betakes him to drive a trade, betweene that and Virginea many yeares. The brethren (sharpe witted) had it spread by and by amongst his freinds in England, that the man was mad. So thought his wife so thought his other freindes, that had it from a Planter of the Towne. So was it thought of those, that did not know, the Brethren could dissemble: why thus they are all of them honest men in their particular, and every man beinge bound to seeke anothers good, shall in the generall doe the best hee can to effect it, and so they may be excused,

I thinke.

A Machivell plot.

The Vaile.

Shipp and goodes confiscated.

When every Conspirator had his share the shipp delivered againe.

Bonds taken not to prosecute.

Report of Mr. Weston was mad in New England.

Honest men in particular.

Chap. VII.

Of Thomas Mortons entertainement at Plimmouth and castinge away upon an Island.

THis man arrived in those parts, and hearing newes of a Towne that was much praised, he was desirous to goe thither, and see how thinges stood, where his entertainement was there best, I dare be bould to say: for although they had but 3. Cowes in all, yet had they fresh butter and a sallet of egges in dainty wise, a dish not common in a wildernes, there hee bestowed some time in the survey of this plantation. His new come servants in the meane time, were tane to taske, to have their zeale appeare, and questioned what preacher was among their company; and finding none, did seeme to condole their estate as if undone, because no man among them had the guift, to be in Ionas steade, nor they the meanes, to keepe them in that path so hard to keepe.

Brave entertainement in the wildernes

The meanes.

Our Master say they reades the Bible and the word of God, and useth the booke of common prayer, but this is not the meanes; the answere is: the meanes, they crie: alas poore Soules where is the meanes, you seeme as if betrayed to be without the meanes: how can you be stayed from fallinge headlonge to perdition? *Facilis descensus averni:* the booke of common prayer sayd they what poore thinge is that, for a man to reade in a booke? No, no, good sirs I would you were neere us, you might receave comfort by instruction: give me a man hath the guiftes of the spirit, not a booke in hand. I doe professe sayes one, to live without the meanes, is dangerous, the Lord doth know.

Book learning despised.

By these insinuations, like the Serpent they did creepe and winde into the good opinion of the illiterate multitude, that were desirous to be freed and gone (to them no doubt, which some of them after confessed) and little good was to be done one them after this charme was used, now plotts and factions, how they might get loose, and here was some 35. stout knaves, & some plotted how to steale Master Westons barque, others exasperated knavishly to worke, would practise how to gett theire Master to an Island; and there leave him, which hee had notice of, and fitted him to try what would be done, and steps aborde his shallop bound for

Villanous plots of knaves.

Cape Anne to the Massachussets, with an Hogshead of Wine, Sugar hee tooke along, the Sailes hoist up and one of the Conspirators aboard to steere, who in the mid way pretended foule weather at the harboure mouth, and therefore for a time, hee would put in to an Island neere, and make some stay where hee thought to tempt his Master to walke the woods, and so be gone but their Master to prevent them, caused the sales and oares to be brought a shore, to make a tilt if neede should be, and kindled fire, broched that Hogshed, and caused them fill the can with lusty liqour, Claret sparklinge neate which was not suffered to grow pale and flatt, but tipled of with quick dexterity, the Master makes a shew of keepinge round, but with close lipps did seeme to make longe draughts, knowinge the wine would make them Protestants, and so the plot was then at large disclosed and discovered, & they made drowsie, and the inconstant windes shiftinge at night did force the kellecke home, and billedge the boat, that they were forced to leave her so, and cut downe trees that grew by the shore, to make Caffes: two of them went over by helpe of a fore saile almost a mile to the maine the other two stayed five dayes after, till the windes would serve to fill the sailes. The first two went to cape Ann by land, and had fowle enough, and fowle wether by the way, the Islanders had fish enough, shel-fish and fire to roast, & they could not perish for lacke of foode, and wine they had to be sure; and by this you see they were not then in any want; the wine and goodes brought thence, the boat left there so billedgd that it was not worth the labor to be mended.

Prevented by discretion.

And discovered in drinke.

The Shallop billedged.

Two men of the Company cast away swim to shore upon trees.

Chap. VIII.

Of the Banishment of Master John Layford, and John Oldum from Plimmouth.

A Minister required to renounce his callinge.

MAster Layford was at the Merchants chardge sent to Plimmouth plantation to be their Pastor: But the Brethren, before they would allow of it, would have him first renounce his calling, to the office of the Ministery, received in England, as hereticall and Papisticall, (so hee confest) and then to receive a new callinge from them, after their fantasticall invention which hee refused, alledging and maintaining, that his calling as it stood was lawfull, and that hee would not renounce it; and so Iohn Oldam his opinion was one the affirmative, and both together did maintaine the Church of England, to be a true Church, although in some particulars (they said) defective concludinge so against the Tenents there, and by this meanes cancelled theire good opinion, amongst the number of the Seperatists, that stay they must not, lest they should be spies, and to fall fowle on this occation, the Brethren thought it would betray their cause, and make it fall under censure, therefore against Master Layford they had found out some scandall; to be laid on his former corse of life, to blemish that, and so to conclude hee was a spotted beast, and not to be allowed, where they ordained to have the Passover kept so zealously: as for Iohn Oldam, they could see hee would be passionate, and moody; and proove himselfe a mad Iack in his mood, and as soone mooved to be moody, and this impatience would Minister advantage to them to be ridd of him.

Impatience confuted by example.

Hanniball when hee had to doe with Fabius, was kept in awe more by the patience of that one enemy, then by the resolution of the whole army: A well tempered enemy is a terrible enemy to incounter. They injoyne him to come to their needeles watch howse in person, and for refusinge give him a cracked Crowne for presse money, and make the blood run downe about his eares, a poore trick, yet a good vaile though Luscus may see thorough it; and for his further behaviour in the Case, proceed to sentence him with banishment, which was performed after a solemne invention in this manner: A lane of Musketiers was made, and hee compelled in scorne to passe along betweene, & to receave a bob upon the bumme be every musketier, and then a board a shallop, and so convayed to Wessaguscus shoare, & staid at Massachussets, to whome Iohn Layford and some few more did resort, where Master Layford freely executed his office and preached every Lords day, and yet maintained his wife & children foure or five, upon his industry there, with the blessing of God, and the plenty of the Land, without the helpe of his auditory, in an honest and laudable manner, till hee was wearied and made to leave the Country.

New Plimmouth presse money.

The Solemnity of banishment.

11

CHAP. IX.

Of a barren doe of Virginea growne fruithfull in New Canaan.

CHildren and the fruit of the Wombe, are said in holy writt, to be an inheritance that commeth of the Lord; then they must be coupled in Gods name first, and not as this and some other have done.

A great happines comes by propagation.

They are as arrowes in the hand of a Gyant; and happy saith David, is the man, that hath his quiver full of them, and by that rule, happy is that Land and blessed to that is apt and fit for increase of children.

I have shewed you before in the second part, of the discourse, how apt it is for the increase of Minerals, Vegetables, and sensible Creatures.

Now I will shew you, how apt New Canaan is like wise for the increase of the reasonable Creatures, Children, of all riches being the principall: and I give you this for an instance.

More Children in New Canaan in 7. yeares, then in Virginea in 27.

This Country of New Canaan in seaven yeares time could show more Children livinge, that have beene borne there, then in 27. yeares could be shewen in Virginea; yet here are but a handful of weomen landed, to that of Virginea.

The Country doth afford such plenty of Lobsters, and other delicate shellfish, and Venus is said to be borne of the Sea, or else it was some sallet herbe proper to the Climate or the fountaine at Weenaseemute made her become teeming here, that had tried a campe royall in other partes, where shee had been & yet never the neere, till shee came in to New Canaan.

Delivered neare Bussards bay. Dead and buried.

Shee was delivered (in a voyage to Virginea) about Bussardes bay, to west of Cape Cod, where shee had a Sonne borne, but died without baptisme and was buried; and being a thinge remarkable, had this Epitaph following made of purpose to memorize the worth of the persons.

EPITAPH.

TIme that brings all thinges to light,
Doth hide th uthinge out of sight,
Yet fame hath left behinde a story,
A hopefull race to shew the glory:

For underneath this heape of stones,
Lieth a percell of small bones,
What hope at last can such impes have,
That from the wombe goes to the grave.

CHAP. X.

Of a man indued with many spetiall guifts sent over to be Master of the Ceremonies.

THis was a man approoved of the Brethren, both for his zeale and guiftes, yet but a Bubble, & at the publike Chardge conveyed to New England, I thinke to be Master of the Ceremonies, betweene the Natives, and the Planters: for hee applied himselfe cheifly to pen the language downe in Stenography: But there for want of use, which hee rightly understood not, all was losse of labor, somethinge it was when next it came to view, but what hee could not tell.

Stenography one guift.

This man Master Bubble was in the time of Iohn Oldams absence made the howse Chaplaine there, and every night hee made use of his guifts, whose oratory luld his auditory fast a sleepe, as Mercuries pipes did Argus eies: for when hee was in; they sayd hee could not tell how to get out: nay hee would hardly out, till hee were fired out, his zeale was such: (one fire they say drives out another,) hee would become a great Merchant, and by any thinge that was to be sold so as hee might have day and be trusted never so litle time: the price it seemed hee stood not much upon, but the day: for to his freind hee shewed commodities so priced, as caused him to blame the buyer, till the man this Bubble did declare, that it was tane up at day, and did rejoyce in the bargaine, insistinge on the day, the day, yea marry quoth his friend if you have doomesday for payment you are then well to passe. But if he had not, it were as good hee had, they were payed all alike.

Oratory another guift.

A great Merchant a third guift.

And now, this Bubbles day is become a common proverbe, hee obtained howse roome at Passonagessit, and removed thether, because it stood convenient, for the Beaver trade, and the rather because the owner of Passonagessit had no Corne left: and this man seemed a bigg boned man, and therefore thought to be a good laborer, and

His day made a common prouerb.

to have store of corne, but contrary wise hee had none at all, and hoped upon this freind his host: thithere were brought the trophies of this Master Bubbles honor: his water tankard and his Porters basket, but no provision, so that one gunne did serve to helpe them both to meat; and now the time for fowle was almost past.

Trophies of honor.

This man and his host at dinner: Bubble begins to say grace yea and a long one to, till all the meate was cold; hee would not give his host leave to say grace, belike hee thought mine host past grace, and further learned as many other Schollers are: but in the usage and custome of this blinde oratory, his host tooke himselfe abused, and the whiles fell to and had halfe done, before this man Bubble would open his eies, to see what stood afore him, which made him more cautius, and learned, that *brevis oratio penetrat Cælum.* Together Bubbles and hee goes in the Canaw to Nut Island for brants, and there his host makes a shotte & breakes the winges of many, Bubble in hast and single handed, paddels out like a Cow in a cage: his host cals back to rowe two handed like to a pare of oares, and before this could be performed, the fowles had time to swimme to other flockes, and so to escape: the best part of the pray being lost, mayd his host to mutter at him, and so to parte for that time discontended.

His long grace made the meat cold.

Chap. XI.

Of a Composition made by the Sachem, for a Theft committed by some of his men shewing their honest meaninge.

THe owner of Passonagessit to have the benefit of company, left his habitation in the Winter and reposed at Wessaguscus, (to his cost) meane time in the Depth of Winter, the neighbour Salvages accustomed to buy foode, came to the howse (for that intent perhaps) & peepinge in all the windowes, (then unglased) espied corne. But no body to sell the same, and having company and helpe at hand, did make a shift to get into the howse, and take out corne to serve but for the present, left enough behinde the Sachem having knowledge of the facte, and being advertised likewise, of the displeasure that had ben

The Salvages betake the howse & take the Corne.

cōceaved, by the Proprietor thereof, at this offence prepares a Messenger, the Salvage that had lived in England, and sends him with commission, for the trespasse of his men who had tenne skinnes perposed for it, to bee payd by a day certaine: The Sachem at the time appointed, bringes the Beaver to Wessaguscus: where the owner lived, but just then was gone abroade, meane time the skinnes were by the Wessaguscus men gelded, & the better halfe by them juggled away: before the owner came, and hee by the Actors perswaded, to bee contended with the rest, who not so pleased did draw the Sachem then to make a new agreement, and so to pay his remnant left in hand, and tenne skinnes more by a new day asigned, and then to bringe them to passonagessit, but the wessaguscus men went the day before to the Salvages with this sayinge, that they were sent to call upon him there for payement, and received tenne skinnes, and tooke a Salvage there to justifie that at their howse; the owner stayed the while, hee verified this, because hee saw the man, before at Wessaguscus: the Sachem did beleive the tale, and at that time delivered up tenne skinnes: On that behalfe, in full dischardge of all demandes, against the trespasse, and the trespassers to them, who consented to him, and them, to the owner, and kept view to themselves, and made the Salvage take the tenth, and give the owner all that yet was to bee had, themselves confessinge their demaunds for him, and that there was but onely one as yet prepared, so that by this you may easily perceive the uncivilized people, are more just then the civilized.

A dishonest tricke.

A consentinge tricke.

The Heathen more just, then the Christians.

Chap. XII.

Of a voyadge made by the Master of the Ceremonies of New Canaan to Neepenett, from whence hee came away, and of the manifold dangers hee escaped.

THis woorthy member Master Bubble, a new Master of the Ceremonies, having a conceipt in his head, that hee had hatched a new device for the purchase of Beaver, beyond Imagination, packes up a sacke full of odde implements, and without any company, but a couple of Indians for guides, (and therefore you may, if you please) beeleive they are so dangerous as the

Two Salvage guides conduct Iohn, to Neepenett alone.

Brethren of Plimmouth give it out, hee betakes him to his progresse into the Inlande for Beaver, with his carriadge on his shoulders like Milo, his guides and hee in processe of time, come to the place appointed, which was about Neepenett, thereabouts being more Beavers to be had then this Milo could carry: And both his journey men, glad hee was good man, and his guides were willing to pleasure him, there the Salvages stay: night came on, but before they were inclined to sleepe, this good man Master Bubble had an evation crept into his head, by misapplying the Salvages actions, that hee must needs be gone in all hast, yea and without his errand, hee purposed to doe it so cunningly that his flight should not be suspected, hee leaves his shooes in the howse, with all his other implements, and flies, as hee was on his way, to increase his feare, suggestinge himselfe that hee was present by a company of Indians, & that there shafts were let fly as thick as haile at him, hee puts of his breeches, and puts them on his head, for to save him from the shafts, that flew after him so thick, that no man could perceave them: and cryinge out avoyd Satan, what have yee to doe with mee, thus running one his way without his breeches, hee was pittifully scratched, with the brush of the underwoods, as hee wandred up and downe in unknowne wayes: The Salvages in the meane time put up all his implements in the sack hee left behinde, and brought them to Wessaguscus, where they thought to have found him; but understanding hee was not returned, were ferefull what to doe: and what would be conceaved of the English was become of this mazed man, the Master of the Ceremonies; and were in consultation of the matter. One of the Salvages was of opinion the English would suppose him to be made away, fearefull hee was to come in sight. The other better acquainted with the English having lived some time in England,) was more confident, and hee perswaded his fellow that the English would be satisfied with relation of the truth, as having had testimony of his fidelity. So they boldly adventured, to shew what they had brougt, and how the matter stood. The English (when the sack was opened) did take a note in writing of all the particulers that were in the sack; & heard what was by the Salvages related of the accidents: but when his shoes were showne, it was thought hee would not have departed without his shoes; and therefore they did conceave that Master Bubble was made away: by some sinister practise of the Salvages, who unadvisedly had bin culpable of a crime which now they sought to excuse; and straightly chardged the Salvages to finde him out againe, and bring him dead, or alive; else their

They take a note of what was in the sack.

wifes and children should be destroyed. The poore Salvages being in a pitifull perplexity, caused their Countrymen to seeke out for this maz'd man; who being in short time found, was brought to Wessaguscus; where hee made a discourse of his travels, and of the perrillous passages: which did seeme to be no lesse dangerous, then these of that worthy Knight Errant, Don Quixote, and how miraculously hee had bin preserved; and in conclusion, lamented the greate losse of his goods, whereby hee thought himselfe undone.

Mr. Bubble must be found againe or else they shall be destroyed.

The perticuler whereof being demaunded, it appeared, that the Salvages had not diminished any part of them; no not so much as one bit of bread: the number being knowne, and the fragments laid together, it appeared all the bisket was preserved, and not any diminished at all: whereby the Master of the Ceremonies was overjoyed, and the whole Company made themselves merry at his discourse of all his perrillous adventures.

Not any thing diminished.

And by this you may observe whether the Salvage people are not full of humanity, or whether they are a dangerous people as Master Bubble and the rest of his tribe would perswade you.

Chap. XIII.

Of a lamentable fit of Mellancolly, that the Barren doe fell into (after the death of her infant, seeing herselfe despised of her Sweete hart,) whereof shee was cured.

WHether this goodly creature of incontinency went to worke upon even termes like Phillis or noe it does not appeare by any Indenture of covenants then extant, whereby shee might legally challenge the performance of any compleate Marriage at his hands, that had bin tradeing with her as Demopheon here to fore had bin with his ostis.

Neverthelesse (for his future advantage) shee indeavoured (like Phillis,) to gaine this Demopheon all to herselfe, who (as it seemes) did meane nothing lesse, by leaving her for the next cōmer, that had any minde to coole his courage by that meanes; the whipping post (as it seemes) at that time not being in publike use, for such kinde of Cony katchers, but seeing herselfe rejected, shee grew into such a passion of Mellancolly, on a sodaine, that it was thought, shee would exhibit a petition for redresse to grim Pluto who had set her a worke, and knowing that the howse of fate has many entrances, shee was pusseld to finde the neerest way. Shee could not resolve on a sodaine: which doore would soonest bring her to his presence handsomely.

Shee cannot one the sodaine resolve which dore to goe in att.

If shee should make way with a knife, shee thought shee might spoyle her drinking in after ages, if by poyson, shee thought it might prolonge her passage thether: if by drowning, shee thought Caron might come the while with his boate, and waft her out of sight: if shee should tie up her complaint in a halter, shee thought the Ropmakers would take exceptions against her good speede. And in this manner shee debated with herselfe, and demurred upon the matter: So that shee did appeare willing enough; but a woman of small resolution.

Which thing when it was publickely knowne, made many come to comfort her. One amongst the rest was by hir requested, on her behalfe, to write to her late unkinde Demopheon. The Gentleman being merrily disposed, in steed of writing an heroicall Epistle, composed this Elegi for a memoriall of some mirth upon the Circumstance of the matter, to be sent unto hir, as followeth:

CARMEN ELEGIACVM.

MElpomene (at whose mischeifous tove,
The screech owles voyce is heard; the mandraks grove)
Commands my pen in an Iambick vaine,
To tell a dismall tale, that may constraine,
The heart of him to bleede that shall discerne,
How much this foule amisse does him concerne,
Alecto (grim Alecto) light thy torch,
To thy beloved sister next the porch,
That leads unto the mansion howse of fate,
Whose farewell makes her freind more fortunate,
A great Squa Sachem can shee poynt to goe,
Before grim Minos, and yet no man know.
That knives, and halters, ponds, and poysonous things,
Are alwayes ready when the Divell once brings,
Such deadly sinners: to a deepe remorse,
Of conscience selfe accusing that will force,
Them to dispaire like wicked Kain, whiles death,
Stands ready with all these to stopp their breadth,
The beare comes by; that oft hath bayted ben,
By many a Satyres whelpe unlesse you can,

Commaund your eies to drop huge milstones forth,
In lamentation of this losse on earth,
Of her, of whome, so much prayse wee may finde,
Goe when shee will, shee'l leave none like behinde,
Shee was too good for earth, too bad for heaven.
Why then for hell the match is somewhat even.

After this, the water of the fountaine at Ma-re Mount, was thought fit to be applyed unto her for a remedy, shee willingly used according to the quality thereof.

And when this Elegy came to be divulged, shee was so conscious of her crime, that shee put up her pipes, and with the next shipp shee packt away to Virginea, (her former habitation) quite cured of her mellancolly with the helpe of the water of the fountaine at Ma-re Mount.

CHAP. XIV.

Of the Revells of New Canaan.

THe Inhabitants of Pasonagessit (having translated the name of their habitation from that ancient Salvage name to Ma-re Mount; and being resolved to have the new name confirmed for a memorial to after ages) did devise amongst themselves to have it performed in a solemne manner with Revels, & merriment after the old English custome: prepared to sett up a Maypole upon the festivall day of Philip and Iacob; & therefore brewed a barrell of excellent beare, & provided a case of bottles to be spent, with other good cheare, for all commers of that day. And because they would have it in a compleat forme, they had prepared a song fitting to the time and present occation. And upon May-day they brought the Maypole to the place appointed, with drumes, gunnes, pistols, and other fitting instruments, for that purpose; and there erected it with the help of Salvages, that came thether of purpose to see the manner of our Revels. A goodly pine tree of 80. foote longe, was reared up, with a peare of buckshorns nayled one, somewhat neare unto the top of it: where it stood as a faire sea marke for directions; how to finde out the way to mine Host of Ma-re Mount.

A Maypole.

And because it should more fully appeare to what end it was placed there, they had a poem in readines made, which was fixed to the Maypole, to shew the new name confirmed upon that plantation; which allthough it were made according to the occurrents of the time, it being Enigmattically composed) pusselled the Seperatists most pittifully to expound it, which (for the better information of the reader) I have here inserted.

THE POEM.

RIse Oedipeus, and if thou canst unfould,
What meanes Caribdis underneath the mould,
When Scilla solitary on the ground,
(Sitting in forme of Niobe) was found;
Till Amphitrites Darling did acquaint,
Grim Neptune with the Tenor of her plaint,
And caused him send forth Triton with the sound,
Of Trumpet lowd, at which the Seas were found,
So full of Protean formes, that the bold shore,
Presented Scilla a new parramore,
So strange as Sampson and so patient,
As Job himselfe, directed thus, by fate,
To comfort Scilla so unfortunate.
I doe professe by Cupids beautious mother,
Heres Scogans choise for Scilla, and none other;
Though Scilla's sick with greife because no signe,
Can there be found of vertue masculine.
Esculapius come, I know right well,
His laboure's lost when you may ring her Knell,
The fatall sisters doome none can withstand,
Nor Cithareas powre, who poynts to land,
With proclamation that the first of May,
At Ma-re Mount shall be kept hollyday.

The man who brought her over was named Samson Iob.

The Maypole called an Idoll the Calfe of Horeb.

The setting up of his Maypole was a lamentable spectacle to the precise seperatists: that lived at new Plimmouth. They termed it an Idoll; yea they called it the Calfe of Horeb: and stood at defiance with the place naming it Mount Dagon; threatning to make it a woefull mount and not a merry mount.

The Riddle for want of Oedipus, they could not expound, onely they made some explication of part of it, and sayd, it was meant by Sampson Iob, the carpenter of the Shipp, that brought over a woman to her husband, that had bin there longe before and thrived so well, that hee sent for her and her children to come to him; where shortly after hee died, having no reason, but because of the sound of those two words: when as (the truth is) the man they applyed it to, was altogether unknowne to the Author.

There was likewise a merry song made, which (to make their Revells more ſashionable) was sung with a Corus, every man bearing his part; which they performed in a daunce, hand in hand about the Maypole, whiles one of the Company sung, and filled out the good liquour like gammedes and Iupiter.

THE SONGE.

DRinke and be merry, merry, merry boyes,
Let all your delight be in the Hymens ioyes,
Jô to Hymen now the day is come,
About the merry Maypole take a Roome.
Make greene garlons, bring bottles out;
And fill sweet Nectar, freely about,
Vncover thy head, and feare no harme,
For hers good liquor to keepe it warme.
Then drinke and be merry, &c.
Iô to Hymen, &c.
Nectar is a thing assign'd,
By the Deities owne minde,
To cure the hart opprest with greife,
And of good liquors is the cheife,
Then drinke, &c.
Iô to Hymen, &c.
Give to the Mellancolly man,
A cup or two of't now and than;
This physick' will soone revive his bloud,
And make him be of a merrier moode.
Then drinke, &c.
Iô to Hymen, &c.
Give to the Nymphe thats free from scorne,
No Irish; stuff nor Scotch over worne,
Lasses in beaver coats come away,
Yee shall be welcome to us night and day.
To drinke and be merry, &c.
Jô to Hymen, &c.

This harmeles mirth made by younge men (that lived in hope to have wifes brought over to them, that would save them a laboure to make a voyage to fetch any over) was much distasted, of the precise Seperatists: that keepe much a doe, about the tyth of Muit and Cummin; troubling their braines more then reason would require about things that are indifferent: and from that time sought occasion against my honest Host of Ma-re Mount to overthrow his ondertakings, and to destroy his plantation quite and cleane. But because they presumed with their imaginary gifts (which they have out of Phaos box) they could expound hidden misteries (to convince them of blindnes as well in this, as in other matters of more cōsequence) I will illustrate the poem, according to the true intent of the authors of these Revells, so much distasted by those Moles.

Oedipus is generally receaved for the absolute reader of riddles who is invoaked: Silla and Caribdis are two dangerous places for seamen to incounter, neere unto vennice, & have bin by poets formerly resembled to man and wife. The like licence the author challenged for a paire of his nomination, the one lamenting for the losse of the other as Niobe for her children. Amphitrite is an arme of the Sea, by which the newes was carried up and downe, of a rich widow, now to be tane up or laid downe. By Triton is the fame spread, that caused the Suters to muster; (as it had bin to Penellope of Greece) and the Coast lying circuler, all our passage to and froe, is made more convenient by Sea, then Land. Many aimed at this marke; but hee that played Proteus best and could comply with her humor must be the man, that would carry her, & hee had need have Sampsons strenght to deale with a Dallila: and as much patience as Iob that should come there, for a thing that I did observe in the life time of the former.

But marriage and hanging (they say) comes by desteny & Scogans choise tis better none at all. Hee that playd Proteus (with the helpe of Priapus) put their noses out of joynt as the Proverbe is.

And this the whole company of the Revellers at Ma-reMount knew to be the true sence and exposition of the riddle: that was fixed to the Maypole, which the Seperatists were at defiance with? some of them affirmed, that the first institution thereof, was in memory of a whore; not knowing that it was a Trophe erected at first, in honor of Maja, the Lady of learning which they despise; vilifying the two universities with uncivile termes; accounting what is there obtained by studdy is but unnecessary learning; not considering that learninge does inable mens mindes to converse with climents of a higher nature then is to be found within the habitation of the

Mole.

Chap. XV.

Of a great Monster supposed to be at Ma-re-Mount; and the preparation made to destroy it.

THe Seperatists envying the prosperity, and hope of the Plantation at Ma-re Mount (which they perceaved beganne to come forward, and to be in a good way for gaine in the Beaver trade) conspired together against mine Host especially, (who was the owner of that Plantation) and made up a party against him; and mustred up what aide they could; accounting of him, as of a great Monster.

Many threatening speeches were given out both against his person, and his Habitation, which they divulged should be consumed with fire: And taking advantage of the time when his company (which seemed little to regard, theire threats) were gone up into the Inlands, to trade with the Salvages for Beaver.

They set upon my honest host at a place, called Wessaguscus, where (by accident) they found him. The inhabitants there were in good hope, of the subvertion of the plantation at Mare Mount, (which they principally aymed at;) and the rather, because mine host was a man that indeavoured to advance the dignity of the Church of England; which they (on the contrary part) would laboure to vilifie; with uncivile termes: enveying against the sacred booke of common prayer, and mine host that used it in a laudable manner amongst his family, as a practise of piety.

There hee would be a meanes to bringe sacks to their mill (such is the thrist after Beaver) and helped the conspiratores to. Surprisee mine host, (who was there all alone) and they chardged him, (because they would seeme to have some reasonable cause against him (to sett a glosse upon their malice) with criminall things which indeede had beene done by such a person but was of their conspiracy; mine host demaunded of the conspirators who it was, that was author of that information, that seemed to be their ground for what they now intended. And because they answered, they would not tell him, hee as peremptorily replyed, that hee would not stay, whether he had, or he had not done as they had bin informed.

The answere made no matter (as it seemed) whether it had bin negatively, or affirmatively made) for they had resolved what hee should suffer, because (as they boasted,) they were now become the greater number: they had shaked of their shackles of servitude, and were become Masters, and masterles people.

It appeares, they were like beares whelpes in former time, when mine hosts plantation was of as much strength as theirs, but now (theirs being stronger,) they (like overgrowne beares) seemed monsterous. In breife, mine host must indure to be their prisoner, untill they could contrive it so, that they might send him for England, (as they said,) there to suffer according to the merrit of the fact, which they intended to father upon him; supposing (belike) it would proove a hainous crime.

Much rejoycing was made that they had gotten their cappitall enemy (as they concluded him) whome they purposed to hamper in such sort, that hee should not be able to uphold his plantation at Ma-re Mount.

The Conspirators sported themselves at my honest host, that meant them no hurt; & were so joccund that they feasted their bodies, and fell to tippeling, as if they had obtained a great prize; like the Trojans when they had the custody of Hippeus pinetree horse.

Mine host fained greefe: and could not be perswaded either to eate, or drinke, because hee knew emptines would be a meanes to make him as watchfull, as the Geese kept in the Roman Cappitall: whereon the contrary part, the conspirators would be so drowsy, that hee might have an opportunity to give them a slip, insteade of a tester. Six persons of the conspiracy were set to watch him at Wessaguscus: But hee kept waking; and in the dead of night (one lying on the bed, for further suerty,) up gets mine Host and got to the second dore that hee was to passe which (notwithstanding the lock) hee got open: and shut it after him with such violence, that it affrighted some of the conspirators.

Mine Host got out of prison.

The word which was given with an alarme, was, ô he's gon, he's gon, what shall wee doe he's gon? the rest (halfe a sleepe) start up in a maze, and like rames, ran theire heads one at another full butt in the darke.

The Captain tore his clothes.

Their grand leader Captaine Shrimp tooke on most furiously, and tore his clothes for anger, to see the empty nest, and their bird gone.

The rest were eager to have torne theire haire from theire heads, but it was so short, that it would give them no hold; Now Captaine Shrimp thought in the losse of this prize (which hee accoumpted his Master peece,) all his honor would be lost for ever.

In the meane time mine Host was got home to Ma-re Mount through the woods, eight miles, round about the head of the river Monatoquit, that parted the two Plantations: finding his way by the helpe of the lightening (for it thundred as hee went terribly) and there hee prepared powther three pounds dried, for his present imployment, and foure good gunnes for him, and the two assistants left at his howse, with bullets of severall sizes three hounderd, or thereabouts; to be used if the conspirators should pursue him thether: and these two persons promised theire aides in the quarrell, and confirmed that promise with a health in good rosa solis.

Mine host got home to Ma-re mount.

Hee provides for his enemies.

Now Captaine Shrimp, the first Captaine in the Land (as hee supposed,) must doe some new act to repaire this losse, and to vindicate his reputation, who had sustained blemish, by this oversight. Begins now to study, how to repaire or survive his honor in this manner; callinge of Councell: they conclude.

Hee takes eight persons more to him, and (like the nine Worthies of New Canaan) they imbarque with preparation against Ma-re-Mount, where this Monster of a man (as theire phrase was) had his denne; the whole number, (had the rest not bin from home, being but seaven,) would have given Captaine Shrimpe (a quondam Drummer,) such a wellcome, as would have made him wish for a Drume as bigg as Diogenes tubb, that hee might have crept into it out of sight.

Now the nine Worthies are approached; and mine Host prepared: having intelligence by a Salvage, that hastened in love from Wessaguscus, to give him notice of their intent.

One of mine Hosts men prooved a craven: the other had prooved his wits to purchase a little valoure, before mine Host had observed his posture.

The nine worthies comming before the Denne of this supposed Monster, (this seaven headed hydra, as they termed him) and began like Don Quixote against the Windmill to beate a party, and to offer quarter (if mine Host would yeald) for they resolved to send him for England, and bad him lay by his armes.

A party.

But hee (who was the Sonne of a Souldier) having taken up armes in his just defence, replyed, that hee would not lay by those armes, because they were so needfull at Sea, if hee should be sent over. Yet (to save the effusion of so much worthy bloud, as would haue issued, out of the vaynes of these 9. worthies of New Canaan, if mine Host should have played upon them out at his port holes (for they came within danger like a flocke of wild geese, as if they had bin tayled one to another, as coults to be sold at a faier) mine Host was content to yeelde upon quarter; and did capitulate with them: in what manner it should be for more certainety, because hee knew what Captaine Shrimpe was.

Captaine Shrimpe promiseth, that no violence should bee offered to his person.

Hee expressed, that no violence should be offered to his person, none to his goods, nor any of his Howsehold: but that hee should have his armes, and what els was requisit for the voyage, (which their Herald retornes,) it was agreed upon, and should be performed.

But mine Host no sooner had set open the dore and issued out: but instantly Captaine Shrimpe, and the rest of the worties stepped to him, layd hold of his armes; and had him downe, and so eagerly was every man bent against him (not regarding any agreement made with such a carnall man,) that they fell upon him, as if they would have eaten him: some of them were so violent, that they would have a slice with scabbert and all for haste, untill an old Souldier (of the Queenes as the Proverbe is) that was there by accident, clapt his gunne under the weapons, and sharply rebuked these worthies for their unworthy practises. So the matter was taken into more deliberate consideration.

The Worthies rebuked for their unworthy practises.

Captaine Shrimpe and the rest of the nine worthies, made themselves (by this outragious riot) Masters of mine Hoste of Ma-re Mount, and disposed of what hee had at his plantation.

This they knew (in the eye of the Salvages) would add to their glory; and diminish the reputation of mine honest Host, whome they practised to be ridd of, upon any termes, as willingly as if hee had bin the very Hidra of the time.

Chap. XVI.

How the 9. worthies put mine Host of Ma-re-Mount into the inchaunted, Castle at Plimmouth, and terrified him with the Monster Briareus.

THe nine Worthies of New Canaan having now the Law in their owne hands (there being no generall Governour in the Land: nor none of the Seperation that regarded, the duety they owe their Soveraigne, whose naturall borne Subjects they were: though translated out of Holland: from whence they had learned to worke all to their owne ends, and make a great shew of Religion, but no humanity, for they were now to sit in Counsell on the cause.

And much it stood mine honest Host upon, to be very circumspect, and to take Eacus to taske: for that his voyce was more allowed of, then both the other: and had not mine Host confounded all the arguments that Eacus could make in their defence: and confuted him that swaied the rest, they would have made him unable to drinke in such manner of merriment any more. So that following this private counsell, given him by one that knew who ruled the rost, the Hiracano ceased that els would split his pinace.

A conclusion was made, and sentence given, that mine Host should be sent to England a prisoner. But when hee was brought to the shipps for that purpose, no man durst be so foole hardy as to undertake carry him. So these Worthies set mine Host upon an Island, without gunne, powther, or shot, or dogge, or so much as a knife, to get any thinge to feede upon or any other cloathes to shelter him with at winter then a thinne suite which hee had one at that time. Home hee could not get to Ma-re-Mount upon this Island. Hee stayed a moneth at least, and was releeved by the Salvages that tooke notice that mine Host was a Sachem of Passonagessit, and would bring bottles of strong liquor to him, and unite themselves into a league of brother hood with mine Host; so full of humanity are these infidels before these Christians.

Mine Host set upon an Island without any thing to shift for himselfe.

From this place for England, sailed mine Host in a Plimmouth shipp, (that came into the Land to fish upon the Coast,) that landed him safe in England at Plimmouth, and hee stayed in England untill the ordinary time for shipping to set forth for these parts; and then retorned: Noe man being able to taxe him of any thinge.

But the Worthies (in the meane time) hoped they had bin ridd of him.

Chap. XVII.

Of the Baccanall Triumphe of the nine worthies of New Canaan.

THe Seperatists were not so contended, (when mine Host of Ma-re-Mount was gone) but they were as much discontended when hee was retorned againe: and the rather, because theire passages about him, and the businesse, were so much derided; and in songes exemplified: which (for better satisfaction of such as are in that kinde affected) I have set forth as it was then in use by the name of the *Baccanall Triumphe*, as followeth:

THE POEM.

Master Ben: Johnson.

I sing th' adventures of mine worthy wights,
And pitty 't is I cannot call them Knights,
Since they had brawne and braine and were right able,
To be installed of Prince Arthures table,
Yet all of them were Squires of low degree,
As did appeare by rules of heraldry,
The Magi tould of a prodigeous birth,
That shortly should be found upon the earth,
By Archimedes art, which they misconster,
Vnto their Land would proove a hiddeous monster.
Seaven heades it had, and twice so many feete,
Arguing the body to be wondrous greate,
Besides a forked taile heav'd up on highe,
As if it threaten'd battell to the skie,
The Rumor of this fearefull prodigy,
Did cause th' effeminate multitude to cry,
For want of great Alcides aide and stood,
Like People that have seene Medusas head,
Great was the greife of hart, great was the mone,
And great the feare conceaved by every one,
Of Hydras hiddeous forme and dreadfull powre,
Doubting in time this Monster would devoure,
All their best flocks whose dainty wolle consorts,
It selfe with Scarlet in all Princes Courts,
Not Iason nor the adventerous youths of Greece,
Did bring from Colcos any richer Fleece,
In Emulation of the Gretian force,
These Worthies nine prepar'd a woodden horse,
And prick'd with pride of like successe divise,
How they may purchase glory by this prize,
And if they give to Hidreas head the fall,
It will remaine a plat forme unto all,
Theire brave atchivements, and in time to comme,
Per fas aut nef as they'l erect a throne.
Cloubs are turne'd trumps: so now the lott is cast,
With fire and sword, to Hidras den they haste,

Mars in th' assendant, Soll in Cancer now,
And Lerna Lake to Plutos court must bow,
What though they rebuk'd by thundering Iove,
Tis neither Gods nor men that can remove,
Their mindes from making this a dismall day,
These nine will now be actors in this play,
And Sum on Hidra to appeare a non,
Before their witles Combination,
But his undaunted spirit nursd with meate,
Such as the Cecrops gave their babe to eate,
Scorn'd their base accons, for with Cecrops charme,
Hee knew he could defend himselfe from harme,
Of Minos, Eacus, and Radamand,
Princes of Limbo who must out of hand,
Consult bout Hidra what must now be done,
Who having sate in Counsell one by one,
Retorne this answere to the Stiggean feinds,
And first grim Minos spake: most loving freinds,
Hidra prognosticks ruine to our state,
And that our Kingdome will grow desolate,
But if one head from thence be tane away,
The Body and the members will decay,
To take in hand, what Eacus this taske,
Is such as barebrained Phaeton did aske,
Of Phebus to begird the world about,
Which graunted put the Netherlands to rout,
Presumptious fooles learne wit at too much cost,
For life and laboure both at once hee lost,
Sterne Radamantus being last to speake,
Made a great hum and thus did silence breake,
What if with ratling chaines or Iron bands,
Hidra be bound either by feete or hands,
And after being lashed with smarting rodds,
Hee be conveyed by Stix unto the godds,
To be accused on the upper ground,
Of Lesæ Majestatis this crime found,
T'will be unpossible from thence I trowe,
Hidra shall come to trouble us belowe,
This sentence pleasd the friends exceedingly,
That up they tost their bonnets and did cry,
Long live our Court in great prosperity.
The Sessions ended some did straight devise,
Court Revells antiques and a world of joyes,
Brave Christmas gambals, there was open hall,
Kept to the full: and sport the Divell and all,

Laboures despised the loomes are laid away,
And this proclaim'd the Stigean Holliday,
In came grim Mino with his motly beard,
And brought a distillation well prepar'd,
And Eacus who is as suer as text,
Came in with his preporatives the next,
Then Radamantus last and principall,
Feasted the Worthies in his sumptuous hall,
There Caron Cerberous and the rout of feinds,
Had lap enough and so their pastims ends.

THE ILLVSTRATIONS.

NOw to illustrate this Poem, and make the sence more plaine, it is to be considered that the Persons at Ma-re-Mount were seaven, and they had seaven heads and 14. feete, these were accounted Hidra with the seaven heads; and the Maypole with the Hornes nailed neere the topp, was the forked tayle of this supposed Monster, which they (for want of skill) imposed: yet feared in time (if they hindred not mine Host) hee would hinder the benefit of their Beaver trade, as hee had done (by meanes of this helpe) in Kyny back river finely, ere they were a wares; who comming too late, were much dismaide to finde that mine Host his boate had gleaned away all beforet hey came; which Beaver is a fitt companion for Scarlett: and I beleeve that Iasons golden Fleece was either the same, or some other Fleece not of so much value.

This action bred a kinde of hart burning in the Plimmouth Planters who after sought occasion against mine Host to overthrowe his undertakings, and to destroy his Plantation, whome they accoumpted a maine enemy to theire Church and State.

Now when they had begunne with him, they thought best to proceede: for asmuch as they thought themselves farre enough from any controule of Iustice; and therefore resolved to be their owne carvers: (and the rather, because they presumed upon some incouragement they had from the favourites of their Sect in England:) and with fire and sword nine in number pursued mine Host; who had escaped theire hands in scorne of what they intended, and betooke him to his habitation in a night of great thunder and lightening, when they durst not follow him, as hardy, as these nine worthies seemed to be.

It was in the Moneth of Iune, that these Marshallists had appointed to goe about this mischeifous project, and deale so crabbidly with mine Host.

After a parly, hee capitulated with them about the quarter, they proffered him, if hee would consent to goe for England, there to answere (as they pretended) some thing they could object against him principall to the generall: But what it would be hee cared not, neither was it any thing materiall.

Yet when quarter was agreed upon, they contrary wise, abused him, and carried him to theire towne of Plimmouth, where (if they had thought hee durst have gone to England) rather then they would have bin any more affronted by him, they would have dispatched him, as Captaine Shrimp in a rage, profest that hee would doe with his Pistoll as mine Host should set his foote into the boate. Howsoever the cheife Elders voyce in that place was more powerfull than any of the rest; who conclude to send mine Host without any other thing to be done to him. And this being the finall agreement, (contrary to Shrimpe and others,) the nine Worthies had a great Feast made, and the furmity pott was provided, for the boats gang by no allowance: and all manner of pastime.

Captaine Shrimpe was so overjoyed in the performance of this exployt; that they had, at that time, extraordinary merriment; a thing not usuall amongst those presisians) and when the winde served, they tooke mine Host into their Shallop; hoysed Saile, and carried him to the Northern parts; where they left him upon a Island.

CHAP. XVIII.

Of a Doctor made at a Commencement in New Canaan

THE Church of Plimmouth having due regard to the weale publike, and the Brethren, that were to come over; and knowing that they would be busily imployed to make provision for the cure of Soules, and therefore might neglect the body for that time: did hold themselves to be in duety bound, to make search for a fitting man that might be able (if so neede requir'd) to take the chardge upon him in that place of imployment: and therefore called a Counsell of the whole Synagoge: amongst which company they choose out a man, that long time had bin nurst up in the tender bosome of the Church: one that had speciall gifts: hee could wright and reade, nay more: hee had tane the oath

A Councell called.

of abjuration, which is a speciall stepp, yea and a maine degree unto perferment, Him they weane: and out of Phaos boxe fitt him with speciall guifts of no lesse worth: they stile him Doctor and forth they send him to gaine imployement and opinion.

What luck is it I cannot hit on his name: but I will give you him by a periphrasis, that you may know him when you meete him next.

Hee was borne at Wrington in the County of Somerset, where hee was bred a Butcher. Hee weares a longe beard, and a Garment like the Greeke that beggd in Pauls Church. This new made Doctor comes to Salem to congratulate: where hee findes some are newly come from Sea, and ill at ease.

Hee takes the patient, and the urinall: vies the State there: findes the Crasis Syptomes, and the attomi natantes: and tells the patient that his disease was winde, which hee had tane by gapeing, feasting, over board at Sea, but hee would quickly ease him of that greife, and quite expell the winde. And this hee did performe, with his gifts hee had: and then hee handled the patient so handsomely, that hee eased him of all the winde, hee had in an instant.

And yet I hope this man may be forgiven, if hee were made a fitting Plant for Heaven.

How hee went to worke with his gifts is a question yet hee did a great cure for Captaine Littleworth, hee cured him of a disease called a wife: and yet I hope this man may be forgiven if shee were made a fitting plant for heaven.

By this meanes hee was allowed 4. p. a moneth, and the chirgeons chest, and made Phisition generall of Salem: where hee exercised his gifts so well, that of full 42. that there hee tooke to cure, there is not one has more cause to complaine, or can say black's his eie. This saved Captaine Littleworths credit, that had truck'd away the vittels: though it brought forth a scandall on the Country by it, and then I hope this man may be forgiven, if they were all made fitting plants for Heaven.

But in mine opinion, hee deserves to be set upon a palfrey, and lead up and downe in triumph throw new Canaan, with a coller of Iurdans about his neck, as was one of like desert in Richard the seconds time through the streets of London, that men might know where to finde a

Quacksaluer.

Chap. XIX.

Of the silencing of a Minister in New Canaan.

A silenced Minister out of courteousnesse, came over into new Canaan to play the spie: Hee pretended out of a zealous intent to doe the Salvages good, and to teach them. Hee brought a great Bundell of Horne books with him, and carefull hee was (good man) to blott out all the crosses of them, for feare least the people of the land should become Idolaters. Hee was in hope, with his gifts, to prepare a great auditory against great Iosua should arive there.

Hee applyed himselfe on the weeke dayes to the trade of Beaver, but it was (as might seeme) to purchase the principall benefite of the Lande, when the time should come; for hee had a hope to be the Caiphas of the Country: and well hee might, for hee was higher by the head than any of his tribe that came after him.

This man, it seemes, played the spie very handsomely, For in the exercise of his guifts on the Lords day at Weenasimute, hee espied a Salvage come in with a good Beaver coate, and tooke occasion to reproove the covetous desire of his auditory to trade for Beaver on those dayes; which made them all use so much modesty about the matter for the present, that hee found opportunity, the same day, to take the Salvage a side into a corner, where (with the helpe of his Wampampeack, hee had in his pocket for that purpose in a readinesse,) hee made a shifte to get that Beaver coate, which their mouthes watered at; and so deceaved them all.

This Caiphas that condemneth Covetousnesse, and committeth it himselfe.

But shortly after, when Iosua came into the Land, hee had soone spied out Caiphas practise; and put him to silence; and either hee must put up his pipes, and be packing or forsake Ionas posture, and play Demas part alltogether.

Chap. XX.

Of the Practise of the Seperatists to gett a snare to hamper mine Host of Ma-re-Mount.

ALthough the nine Worthies had left mine Hoste upon an Island, in such an inhumane manner, as yee heard before; yet when they understood that hee had got shipping, and was gone to England of his owne accord, they dispatched letters of advise to an Agent they had there: and by the next shipp sent after, to have a snare made, that might hamper mine Host so, as hee might not any more trouble theire conscience: and to that end, made a generall collection of Beaver to defray the chardge, and hee was not thought a good Christian that would not lay much out for that imployment.

The generall collection made.

Some contributed three pounds; some foure, some five pounds, and procured a pretty quantity by that Devise, which should be given to a cunning man, that could make a snare to hamper him.

The Agent (according to his direction,) does his endeavoure (in the best manner hee could) to have this instrument made: and used no little diligence to have it effected. His reputation stood upon the taske imposed upon him against mine Host, the onely enemy (accounted) of their Church, and State.

Noe cost spared for the getting of a skillfull man.

Much inquiry was made in London, and about, for a skillfull man that would worke the feate. Noe cost was spared, for gold hee had good store, first hee inquires of one: and then another: at the last hee heard newes of a very famous man, one that was excellent at making subtile instruments such as that age had never bin acquainted with.

Hee was well knowne to be the man, that had wit and wondrous skill, to make a cunning instrument, where with to save himselfe, and his whole family: if all the world besides should be drown'd; and this the best, yea and the best cheap too; for no good done, the man would nothing take.

To him this agent goes, and praies his aide: Declares his cause, & tells the substance of his greivance, all at large, and laid before his eies a heape of gold.

The heape of gold.

When all was shewd, that could be she'd, and said what could be said, & all too little for to have it done; the agent then did see his gold refused, his cause despised & thought himselfe disgraced, to leave the worke undone: so that hee was much dismaid, yet importun'd the cunning, who found no reason to take the taske in hand.

Hee thought perhaps, mine Host (that had the slight to escape from the nine Worthies, to chaine Argus eies, and by inchauntment make the doores of the watch tower fly open at an instant) would not be hampered, but with much a doe: and so hee was unwilling to be troubled with that taske.

The agent wondring to see that his gold would doe no good, did aske, the cunning man if hee could give him no advise?

who said, hee would: and what was that thinke you? To let mine Host alone, who being ship'd againe for the parts of New Canaan, was put in at Plimmouth in the very faces of them, to their terrible amazement to see him at liberty, and told him hee had not yet fully answered the matter, they could object against him. Hee onely made this modest reply, that hee did perceave they were willfull people, that would never be answered; and derided them for their practises and losse of laboure.

Mine Hoost arrived again in Plimmouth.

Chap. XXI.

Of Captaine Littleworth his new devise for the purchase of Beaver.

IN the meane time, whiles these former passages were: There was a great swelling fellow, of Littleworth, crept over to Salem (by the helpe of Master Charter party the Tresorer, and Master Ananias increase the Collector for the Company of Seperatists,) to take upon him their imployments for a time.

Charter party Treasorer.

Hee resolving to make hay, whiles the Sonne did shine, first pretended himselfe to be sent over as cheife Iustice of the Massachussets Bay, and Salem forsoth, and tooke unto him a councell & a worthy one no doubt; For the Cowkeeper of Salem, was a prime man in those imployments; and to ad a Majesty (as hee thought) to his new assumed dignity, hee caused the Patent of the Massachussets (new brought into the Land) to be carried where hee went in his progresse to and froe, as an embleme of his authority: which the vulger people not acquainted with, thought it to be some instrument of Musick locked up in that covered case, and thought (for so some said) this man of littleworth had bin a fidler, and the rather, because hee had put into the mouthes of poore silly things that were sent a longe with him, what skill hee had in Engines and in things of quaint devise: all which prooved in conclusion to be but impostury.

This man thinking none so worthy as himselfe, tooke upon him infinitely: and made warrants in his owne name (without relation to his Majesties authority in that place,) and summoned a generall apparance, at the worshipfull towne of Salem: there is open assembly

Warrants made by Capt. Littleworth in his name.

was tendered certaine Articles, devised betweene him and their new Pastor Master Eager (that had renounced his old calling to the Ministry receaved in England, by warrant of Gods word: and taken a new one there by their fantasticall way imposed and conferred upon him with some speciall guifts had out of Phaos boxe.)

To these Articles every Planter, old, and new, must signe: or be expelled from any manner of aboade within the Compas of the Land contained within that graunt then shewed: which was so large, it would suffice for Elbow roome, for more then were in all the Land by 700000. such an army might have planted them a Colony with that cirquit which hee challenged, and not contend for roome for their Cattell. But for all that, hee that should refuse to subscribe, must pack.

The tenor of the *Articles* were these: *That in all causes as well Ecclesiasticall, as Polititicall, wee should follow the rule of Gods word.*

Mine Host subscribed not.

This made a shew of a good intent, and all the assembly (onely mine Host replyed) did subscribe: hee would not unlesse they would ad this Caution: *So as nothing be done contrary, or repugnant to the Lawes of the Kingdome of England.* These words hee knew, by former experience, were necessary, and without these, the same would proove a very mousetrapp to catch some body by his owne consent, (which the rest nothing suspected) for the construction of the worde would be made by them of the Seperation, to serve their owne turnes: and if any man should, in such a case be accused of a crime (though in it selfe it were petty) they might set it on the tenter hookes of their imaginary gifts and stretch it, to make it seeme cappitall; which was the reason why mine Host refused to subscribe.

The Patent.

It was then agreed upon, that there should be one generall trade used within that Patent (as hee said) and a generall stock: and every man to put in a parte: and every man, for his person, to have shares alike: and for their stock according to the ratable proportion was put in: and this to continue for 12. moneths: and then to call an accompt.

All consented but my Host.

All were united but mine Host refused: two truckmasters were chosen; wages prefixed; onely mine Host put in a Caviat, that the wages might be payed but of the cleare proffit, which there in black and white was plainely put downe.

But before the end of 6. moneths, the partners in this stock (handled by the Truckmasters) would have an accompt: some of them had perceaved that Wampambeacke could be pocketted up, and the underlings (that went in the boats alonge) would be neere the Wiser for any thinge, but what was trucked for Beaver onely.

The accoumpt being made betweene Captaine Littleworth, and the two Truckmasters; it was found, that instead of increasing the proffit, they have decreased it; for the principall stock, by this imployment, was freetted so, that there was a great hole to be seene in the very middle of it which cost the partners afterwards one hundred markes to stopp, and make good to Captaine Littleworth.

Instead of proffit disproffit.

But mine Host that sturred not his foote at all for the matter, did not onely save his stock from such a Cancar, but gained sixe and seaven for one: in the meane time, hee derided the Contributers for being catch'd in that snare.

Chap. XXII.

Of a Sequestration made in New Canaan.

Captaine Littleworth (that had an akeing tooth at mine Host of Ma-re-Mount,) devised how hee might put a trick upon him, by colour of a Sequestration, and got some persons to pretend that hee had corne, and other goods of theirs in possession; and the rather, because mine Host had store of corne; and hee had improvidently truckt his store, for the present gaine of Beaver: in so much that his people under his chardge were put to short allowance; which caused some of them to sicken with conceipt of such useage: and some of them (by the practise of the new entertained Doctor Noddy, with his Imaginary gifts: They sent therefore to exhibit a petition to grim Minos, Eacus, and Radamant: where they wished to have the author of their greife to be converted: and they had procured it quickly: if curses would have caused it: for good prayers would be of no validity (as they supposed) in this extremity.

Now in this extremity Capt. Littleworth gave commission to such as hee had found ready for such imployments, to enter in the howse at Ma-re-Mount, and with a shallop, to bring from thence such corne, and other utensilles, as in their commission hee had specified. But mine Host, wary to prevent eminent mischeife, had conveyed his powther, and shott (and such other things as stood him in most steed for his present condition) into the woods for safety: &

Commission for corne.

whiles this was put in practise by him, the shallop was landed, and the Commissioners entred the howse; and willfully bent against mine honest Host, that loved good hospitality. After they had feasted their bodies with that they found there, they carried all his corne away, with some other of his goods, contrary to the Lawes of hospitality: a smale parcell of refuse corne onely excepted, which they left mine Host to keepe Christmas with.

Mine Hosts corne & goods carried away by violence.

But when they were gone, mine Host, fell to make use of his gunne, (as one that had a good faculty in the use of that instrument) and feasted his body neverthelesse with fowle, and venison, which hee purchased with the helpe of that instrument: the plenty of the Country, and the commodiousnes of the place affording meanes by the blessing of God; and hee did but deride Captaine Littleworth, that made his servants snap shorte in a Country so much abounding with plenty of foode for an industrious man, with great variety.

Chap. XXIII.

Of a great Bonfire made for ioy of the arrivall of great Iosua surnamed Temperwell into the Land of Canaan.

SEaven shipps set forth at once, and altogether arrived in the Land of Canaan, to take a full possession thereof: What are all the 12. Tribes of new Israell come: No, none but the tribe of Issacar; and some few scattered Levites of the remnant of those that were descended of old Elies howse.

And here comes their Iosua too among them and they make it a more miraculous thing for these seaven shipps to set forth together, and arrive at New Canaan together, then it was for the Israelites to goe over Iordan drishod: perhaps it was, because they had a wall on the right hand and a wall on the left hand.

These Seperatists suppose there was no more difficulty in the matter, then for a man to finde the way to the Counter at noone dayes, betweene a Sergeant and his yeoman: Now you may thinke mine Host will be hamperd or never.

Men that come to rid the land of pollution.

These are the men that come prepared to ridd the Land, of all pollution. These are more subtile, then the Cunning, that did refuse a goodly heap of gold. These men have brought a very snare indeed;

and now mine Host must suffer. The book of Common Prayer which hee used to be despised: and hee must not be spared.

Now they are come, his doome before hand was concluded on: they have a warrant now: A cheife one too; and now mine Host must know hee is the subject of their hatred: the Snare must now be used; this instrument must not be brought by Iosua in vaine.

A Court is called of purpose for mine host; hee there convented: and must heare his doome, be-fore hee goe: nor will they admitt him to capitulate, and know wherefore they are so violent to put such things in practise against a man they never saw before: nor will they allow of it, though hee decline their Iurisdiction.

A Courte called about mine Host.

There they are all with one assent put him to silence, crying out, heare the Governour, heare the Govern: who gave this sentence against mine Host at first sight: that he should be first put in the Billbowes, his goods should be all confiscated; his Plantation should be burned downe to the ground, because the habitation of the wicked should no more appeare in Israell; and his person banished from those territories, and this put in execution with all speede.

A divellish sentance against him

The harmeles Salvages (his neighboures) came the while, greived poore silly lambes: to see what they went about; and did reproove these Eliphants of witt for their inhumane deede the Lord above did opon their mouthes like Balams Asse, & made them speake in his behalfe sentences, of unexpected divinity, besides morrallity; and tould them, that god would not love them, that burned this good mans howse: and plainely sayed, that they who were new come would finde the want of such a howses in the winter; so much themselves to him confest.

The Salvages reproove them.

The smoake that did assend appeared to be the very Sacrifice of Kain. Mine Host (that a farre of abourd a ship did there behold this wofull spectacle,) knew not what hee should doe, in this extremity; but beare and forbeare, as Epictetus sayes: it was bootelesse to exclaime.

Epictetus summa totius philosophiae.

Hee did consider then, these transitory things are but *ludibria fortunæ* as Cicero calls them. All was burnt downe to the ground, and nothing did remaine, but the bare ashes as an embleme of their cruelty: and unles it could (like to the Phenix) rise out of these ashes, and be new againe, (to the immortall glory and renowne, of this fertile Canaan the new, the stumpes and postes in their black liveries will mourne; and piety it selfe will add a voyce to the bare remnant of that Monument, and make it cry for recompence (or else revenge) against the Sect of cruell Schismaticks.

Chap. XXIV.

Of the digrading and creating gentry in New Canaan.

THere was a zealous Professor in the Land of Canaan (growne a great Merchant in the Beaver trade) that came over for his conscience sake, (as other men have done) and the meanes; (as the phrase is) who in his minority had bin prentice to a tombe maker; who comming to more ripenes of yeares (though lesse discretion,) found a kind of scruple in his conscience, that the trade was in parte against the second commandement: and therefore left it off wholely, and betooke himselfe to some other imployments.

An Elder.

In the end hee settled upon this course: where hee had hope of preferrement, and become one of those things that any Iudas might hange himselfe upon, that is an Elder.

Hee had bin a man of some recconing in his time (as himselfe would boast) for hee was an officer, just under the Ex Chequer at Westminister, in a place called Phlegeton: there hee was comptroller, and conversed with noe plebeians I tell you: but such as have angels or their attendance, (I meane some Lawyers, with appertenances (that is Clarks,) with whome a lugg of Beare, and a crusty rolle in the terme, is as currant as a three penny scute at Hall time.

There is another place, thereby called sticks: these are to two daingerous places, by which the infernall gods do sweare: but this of Sticks is the more daingerous of the two, because there, (if a man be once in) hee cannot tell how to get out againe handsomely.

I knew an under sheriff was in unwaires, and hee laboured to be free of it: yet hee broake his back before hee got so farre as quietus est: There is no such danger in Phlegeton, where this man of so much recconing was comptroller.

Iosua displeased.

Hee being here, waited an opportunity to be made a gentl. and, now it fell out that a gent. newly come into the land of Canaan (before hee knew what ground hee stood upon) had incurred the displeasure of great Iosua so highly, that hee must therefore be digraded.

No reconciliation could be had for him: all hopes were past

for that matter: Where upon this man of much recconing) pretending a graunt of the approach in avoydance) helpes the lame dogge over the stile; and was as jocund on the matter as a Magpie over a Mutton.

Wherefore the Heralls with Drums, and Trumpets, proclaiming in a very solemne manner, that it was the pleasure of great Iosua (for divers and sundry very good causes and considerations, Master Temperwell there unto especially mooving) to take away the title, prerogative and preheminence of the Delinquent, so unworthy of it, and to place the same upon a Professor of more recconing: so that it was made a penall thing for any man after, to lifte the same man againe on the top of that stile; but that hee should stand perpetually digraded from that prerogative. And the place by this meanes being voyde, this man of so much more reckoning, was receaved in like a Cypher to fill up a roome, and was made a Gentleman of the first head; and his Coate of Armes blazon'd and tricked out fit for that purpose, in this Poem following.

Master Temperwell.

THE POEM.

WHat ailes Pigmalion? Is it Lunacy;
Or Doteage on his owne Imagery?
Let him remember how hee came from Hell,
That after ages by record may tell,
The Compleate story to posterity;
Blazon his Coate in forme of Heraldry;
Hee beareth argent alwaies at commaund; *Put it this way.*
A barre betweene three crusty rolls at hand:
And for his crest with froth there does appeare,
Dextra Paw Elevant a lugg of beare.

Now that it may the more easily be understood, I have here endeavoured to set it forth in these illustrations following Pigmalion was an Image maker, who doteing on his owne perfection in making the Image of Venus, grew to be amazed man, like our Gentleman here of the first head: and by the figure Antonomasia is hee herein exemplified.

Hee was translated from a tombe maker, to be the tapster at hell (which is in Westminister under the Ex-Chequer office (for the benefit of the meanes) hee translated himselfe into New England: whereby the help of Beaver and the command of a servent or two, hee was advaunced to the title of a gentleman; where I left him to the exercise of his guifts.

Chap. XXV.

Of the manner how the Seperatists doe pay debts to them that are without.

THere was an honest man, one Mr. Innocence Fairecloath by Mr. Mathias Charterparty, sent over into New Canaan, to raise a very good marchantable commodity for his benefit; for whiles the man was bound by covenant to stay for a time, and to imploy such servants, as did there belong to Mr. Charterparty. Hee disdained the tenents of the Seperatists: and they also (finding him to be none,) disdained to be imployed by a carnall man (as they termed him) and sought occasion against him, to doe him a mischeife, intelligence was conveyed to Mr. Charterparty, that this man was a member of the Church of England: and therefore (in their account) an enemy to their Church, & state. And (to the end they might have some coloure against him) some of them practised to get into his debte; which hee not mistrusting) suffered: and gave credit for such commodity as hee had sold at a price. When the day of payment came, insteede of monyes; hee being at that time sick and weake, and stood in neede of the Beaver hee had contracted for hee, had an Epistle full of zealous exhortations, to provide for the soule, and not to minde these transitory things that perished with the body; and to be thinke himselfe whether his conscience would be so prompt to demaund so greate a somme of Beaver as had bin contracted for. Hee was further exhorted therein to consider hee was but a steward for a time, and by all likely hood was going to give up an accompt of his steward ship: and therfore perswaded the creditor not to load his conscience with such a burthen, which hee was bound by the Gospell to ease him of (if it were possible) & for that cause hee had framed this Epistle in such a freindly manner to put him in minde of it. The perusall of this (lap'd in the paper) was as bad as a potion, to the creditor, to see his debtor Master Subtilety a zealous professor (as hee thought) to deride him in this extremity, that hee could not chuse (in admiration of the deceipt) but cast out these words:

Good Payement.

Are these youre members? if they be all like these I beleeve the Divell was the setter of their Church.

This was called in question, when Mr. Fairecloath least

thought of it. Capt. Littleworth must be the man must presse it against him, for blasphemy against the Church of Salem: and to greate Iosua Temperwell hee goes with a bitter accusation, to have Master Innocence made an example for all carnall men, to presume to speake the least word that might tend to the dishonor of the Church of Salem; yea the mother Church of all that holy Land.

Blasphemy an example for carnall men.

And hee convented was before their Synagoge, where no defence would serve his turne, yet was there none to be seene to accuse him, save the Court alone.

The time of his sicknes, nor the urgent cause, were not allowed to be urg'd for him; but whatsoever could be thought upon against him was urged, seeing hee was a carnall man of them, that are without. So that it seemes by those proceedings there the matter was adjudged before he came: Hee onely brought to heare his sentence in publicke: which was, to have his tongue bored through; his nose slit; his face branded; his eares cut; his body to be whip'd in every severall plantation of theire Iurisdiction: and a fine of forty pounds impo'd with perpetuall banishment: and (to execute this vengeance) shackles (the Deacon of Charles Towne) was as ready as Mephostophiles, when Doctor Faustus was bent upon mischeife.

Hee is the purser generall of New Canaan, who (with his whipp, with knotts most terrible) takes this man unto the Counting howse: there capitulates with him, why hee should be so hasty for payment, when Gods deare children must pay as they are able: and hee weepes, and sobbes, and his handkercher walkes as a signe of his sorrow for Master Fairecloaths sinne, that hee should beare no better affection to the Church and the Saints of New Canaan: and strips innocence the while and comforts him.

Though hee be made to stay for payment, hee should not thinke it longe; the payment would be sure when it did come, and hee should have his due to a doite; hee should not wish for a token more; And then tould it him downe in such manner, that hee made Fairecloaths Innocent back, like the picture of Rawhead and blowdy bones: and his shirte like pudding wifes aperon. In this imployment shackles takes a greate felitity, and glories in the practise of it: This cruell sentence was stoped, in part by Sir Christopher Gardiner (then present at the execution) by expostulating with Master Temperwell: who was content (with that whipping, and the cutting of parte of his eares) to send Innocence going, with the losse of all his goods to pay the fine imposed, and

Notable Pay.

perpetuall banishment out of their Lands of New Canaan in terrorem populi.

Loe this is the payment you shall get, if you be one of them they terme, without.

Chap. XXVI.

Of the Charity of the Seperatists.

CHarity is sayd to be the darling of Religion and is indeed the Marke of a good Christian: But where we doe finde a Commission for ministring to the necessity of the Saints, we doe not finde any prohibition against casting our bread upon the waters, were the unsanctified, as well as the sanctified, are in possibility to make use of it.

I cannot perceave that the Seperatists doe allowe of helping our poore though they magnify their practise in contributing to the nourishment of their Saints For as much as some that are of the number of those whom they terme without (though it were in case of sicknesse) upon theire landing, when a little fresh victuals would have recovered their healths, yet could they not finde any charitable assistance from thē. Nay mine Host of Ma-re-Mount (if hee might have had the use of his gunne powther, and shott, and his dogg: which were denied) hee doubtles would have preserved, such poore helples wretches as were neglected by those that brought them over; which was so apparant (as it seemed) that one of their owne tribe said: death of them would be required at some bodies hands one day, (meaning Master Temperwell.

Lame charity.

But such good must not come from a carnall man: if it come from a member, then it is a sanctified worke; if otherwise, it is rejected, as unsanctified.

But when shackles wife, and such as had husbands parents, or freinds happened to bee sick, mine Hosts helpe was used, and instruments provided for him, to kill fresh vittell with (wherein hee was industrious) and the persons, having fresh vittell, lived.

So doubtles might many others have bin preserved, but they were of the number left without; neither will those precise people admit a carnall man into their howses, though they have made use of his in the like case, they are such antagonists to those, that doe not comply with them and seeke to be admitted, to be of their Church that in scorne they say: you may see what it is to be without.

CHAP. XXVII.

Of the practise of their Church.

THe Church of the Seperatists, is governed by Pastors, Elders, and Deacons, and there is not any of these (though hee be but a Cow keeper) but is allowed to exercise his guifts, in the publik assembly on the Lords day; so as hee doe not make use of any notes for the helpe of his memory: for such things they say smell of Lampe oyle, and there must be no such unsavery perfume admitted, to come into the congregation.

These are all publike preachers. There is amongst these people a Deakonesse made of the sisters, that uses her guifts at home in an assembly of her sexe, by way of repetition, or exhortation: such is their practise.

The Pastor (before hee is allowed of) must disclaime his former calling to the Ministry, as hereticall; and take a new calling after their fantasticall inventions: and then hee is admitted to bee their Pastor.

The manner of disclaimeing is, to renounce his calling with bitter execrations, for the time that hee hath heretofore lived in it: and after his new election, there is great joy conceaved at his commission.

And theire Pastors have this preheminence above the Civile Magistrate: Hee must first consider of the complaint, made against a member: and if hee be disposed to give the partie complained of, an admonition, there is no more to be said: if not; Hee delivers him over to the Magistrate to deale with him in a course of Iustice, according to theire practise, in cases of that nature.

Of these pastors I have not knowne many: some I have observed; together with their carriage in New Canaan: and can informe you what opinion hath bin conceaved of theire conditions in the perticuler. There is one who (as they give it out there, that thinke they speake it to advance his worth) has bin expected to exercise his gifts in an assembly, that stayed his comming, (in the middest of his Iorney) falls into a fitt (which they terme a zealous meditation) and was 4. miles past the place appointed before hee came to himselfe, or did remember where abouts hee went. And how much these things are different from the actions of mazed men, I leave to any indifferent man to judge; and if I should say, they are all much alike, they that have seene and heard, what have done will not condemne mee altogether.

Now for as much as by the practise of their Church every Elder or Deacon may preach: it is not amisse to discover their practise in that perticuler, before I part with them.

It has bin an old saying, and a true, what is bred in the bone will not out of the flesh, nor the stepping into the pulpit that can make the person fitt for the imployment. The unfitnes of the person undertaking to be the Messenger, has brought a blemish upon the message, as in the time of Lewes the Eleventh King of France; who (having advaunced his Barber to place of Honor, and graced him with eminent titles) made him so presumptuous, to undertake an Embassage to treat with forraine princes of Civile affaires.

Lewes the II. sent a Barber Embassador.

But what was the issue? Hee behaved himselfe unworthily (yet as well as his breeding would give him leave) that both the Messenger and the message were despised; and had not hee (being discovered) conveyed himselfe out of their territories, they had made him pay for his barbarous presumption.

The Embassage despised.

Socrates sayes, *loquere ut te videam.* If a man observe these people in the exercise of their gifts, hee may thereby discerne the tincture of their proper calling, the asses eares will peepe through the lyons hide. I am sorry they cannot discerne their owne infirmities I will deale fairely with them; for I will draw their pictures cap a pe, that you may discerne them plainely from head to foote in their postures that so much bewitch (as I may speake with modesty,) these illiterate people to be so fantasticall, to take Ionas taske upon them without sufficient warrant.

A Grocer.

One steps up like the Minister of Iustice with the ballance onely, not the sword for feare of affrighting his auditory. Hee poynts at a text, and handles it as evenly as hee can; and teaches the auditory, that the thing hee has to deliver; must be well waied, for it is a very pretious thing, yet much more pretious then gold, or pearle: and hee will teach them the meanes how to way things of that excellent worth: that a man would suppose, hee, and his auditory were to part stakes by the scale; and the like distribution they have used about a bag pudding.

A Taylor.

Another (of a more cutting disposition) steps in his steed; and hee takes a text, which hee divides into many parts: (to speake truly) as many as hee list. The fag end of it hee pares away, as a superfluous remnant.

Hee puts his auditory in comfort, that hee will make a garment for them: and teach them how they shall put it on; and incourages them to be in love with it. for it is of such a fashion as doth best become a Christian man. Hee will assuer them that it shall be armor of proffe against all assaults of Satan. This garment (sayes hee) is not composed as the garments made by a carnall man, that are sowed with a hot needle, and a burning thread; but it is a garment that shall out last all the garments: and (if they will make use of it, as hee shall direct them) they shall be able (like saint George) to terrifie the greate Dragon error; and defend truth which error with her wide chaps, would devoure: whose mouth shall be filled with the shredds, and parings, which hee continually gapes for under the cutting bourd.

A Tapster.

A third, hee supplies the rome: and in the exercise of his guifts begins with a text that is drawne out of a fountaine, that has in it no dreggs of popery. This shall proove unto you (says hee) the Cup of repentance, it is not like unto the Cup of the Whore of Babilon, who will make men drunk with the dreggs thereof: It is filled up to the brim with comfortable joyce, and will proove a comfortable cordiall to a sick soule, (sayes hee,) And so hee handles the matter as if hee dealt by the pinte, and the quarte with Nic and Froth.

A Cobler.

An other (a very learned man indeed) goes another way to worke with his auditory; and exhorts them to walke upright, in the way of their calling, and not (like carnall men) tread awry. And if they should fayle in the performance of that duety, yet they should seeke for amendement whiles it was time; and tells them, it would bee to late to seek for help, when the shop windowes were shutt up: and pricks them forward with a freindly admonition, not to place theire delight in worldly pleasures, which will not last, but in time will come to an end.

But so to handle the matter, that they may be found to wax better and better, and then they shall be doublely rewarded for theire worke: and so closes up the matter in a comfortable manner.

But stay: Here is one stept up in haste, and (being not minded to hold his auditory in expectation of any long discourse,) hee takes a text; and (for brevities sake,) divides it into one part: and then runnes so fast a fore with the matter, that his auditory cannnot follow him. Doubtles his Father was some Irish footeman, by his speede it seemes so. And it may be at the howre of death, the sonne being present) did participat of his Fathers nature, (according to Pi-

A very patorick.

thagoras) and the vertue of his Fathers nimble feete (being infused into his braines) might make his tongue outrunne his wit.

Well, if you marke it, these are speciall gifts indeede: which the vulgar people are so taken with, that here is no perswading them that it is so rediculous.

This is the meanes, (O the meanes,) that they pursue: This that comes without premeditation: This is the Suparlative: and hee that does not approove of this, they say is a very reprobate.

Many unwarrantable Tenents they have likewise: some of which being come to my knowledge I wil here set downe, one wherof being in publicke practise maintained, is more notorious then the rest. I will therefore beginne with that and convince them of manifest error by the maintenance of it, which is this:

Tenent I. That it is the Magistrates office absolutely (and not the Ministers) to joyne the people in lawfull matrimony. And for this they vouch the History of Ruth, saying Boas was married to Ruth in presence of the Elders of the people. Herein they mistake the scope of the text.

2. That it is a relique of popery to make use of a ring in marriage: and that it is a diabolicall circle for the Divell to daunce in.

3. That the purifications used for woemen after delivery is not to be used.

4. That no child shall be baptised, whose parents are not receaved into their Church first.

5. That no person shall be admitted to the Sacrament of the Lords supper that is without.

6. That the booke of Common prayer is an idoll: and all that use it, Idolaters.

7. That every man is bound to beleeve a professor upon his bare affirmation onely, before a Protestant upon oath.

8. That no person hath any right to Gods creatures, but Gods children onely who are themselves: and that all others are but usurpers of the Creatures.

9. And that for the generall good of their Church, and commonwealth they are to neglect father, mother and all freindship.

10. Much a doe they keepe about their Church discipline, as if that were the most essentiall part of their Religion, Tythes are banished from thence, all except the tyth of Muit and Commin.

11. They differ from us some thing in the creede too, for if they get the goods of one, that is without, into their hands; hee shall be kept without remedy for any satisfaction: and they beleeve, that this is not cosenage.

12. And lastly they differ from us, in the manner of praying;

for they winke when they pray, because they think themselves so perfect in the highe way to heaven, that they can find it blindfould: so doe not I.

Chap. XXVIII.

Of their Policy in publik Iustice.

NOw that I have anottomized, the two extreame parts of this Politique Commonwealth the head & the inferior members, I will shew you the hart & reade a short lecture over that too; which is Iustice.

I have a petition to exhibit to the highe & mighty M^r^. Temperwell; and I have my choise whether I shall make my plaint in a case of conscience, or bring it with in the Compas of a point in law. And because I will goe the surest way to worke, at first, I will see how others are answered in the like kinde, whether it be with hab or nab, as the Iudge did the Countryman.

Here comes M^r^. Hopewell: his petition is in a case of conscience (as hee sayes.) But see great Iosua allowes conscience to be of his side: yet cuts him off; with this answere; Law is flat against him. Well let me see another. I marry: Here comes one Master doubt not: his matter depends (I am sure) upon a point in Law: alas what will it not doe, looke ye it is affirmed that Law is on his side: but Conscience (like a blanket over) spreades it. This passage is like to the Procustes of Roome mee thinks: and therefore I may very well say of them.

Even so by racking out the joynts & chopping of the head,
Procusles fitted all his guests unto his Iron bedd.

And if these speede no better, with whome they are freinds, that neither finde Law nor Conscience to helpe them: I doe not wonder to see mine Host of Ma-re-Mount speede so ill, that has bin proclaimed an enemy so many yeares in New Canaan to their Church and State.

Chap. XXIX.

How mine Host was put into a whales belly.

THe Seperatists (after they had burned Ma-re-Mount, they could not get any shipp to undertake the carriage of mine Host from thence, either by faire meanes, or fowle,) they were inforced (contrary to their expectation) to be troubled with his company: and by that meanes had time to consider more of the man, then they had done of the matter: wherein at length it was discovered, that they by meanes of their credulity of the intelligence given them in England of the matter, and the false Carecter of the man) had runne themselves headlonge into an error: and had done that on a sodaine, which they repented at leasure: but could not tell which way to help it as it stood now. They could debate upon it; and especially upon two difficult points, whereof one must be concluded upon. If they sent mine Host a way by banishment, hee is in possibility to survive, to their disgrace for the injury done: if they suffer him to stay, & put him in *statu quo prius*, all the vulgar people will conclude they have bin too rashe in burning a howse that was usefull, and count them men unadvised.

So that it seemes (by theire discourse about the matter) they stood betwixt Hawke and Bussard: and could not tell which hand to incline unto. They had sounded him secretly: hee was content with it, goe which way it would. Nay shackles himselfe, (who was imployed in the burning of the howse, and therefore feared to be caught in England) and others were so forward in putting mine Host *in statu quo prius*, after they had found their error, (which was so apparent that Luceus eies would have served to have found it out in lesse time) that they would contribute 40. shillings a peece towards it; and affirmed, that every man according to his ability that had a hand in this black designe should be taxed to a Contribution in like nature: it would be done exactly.

Now (whiles this was in agitation, & was well urged by some of those partys, to have bin the up shot) unexpected (in the depth of winter, when all shipps were gone out of the land) In comes Mr. Wethercock a proper Mariner; and they said; he could observe the winde: blow it high, blow it low, hee was resolved to lye at hull rather than incounter such a storme as mine Host had met with: and this was a man for their turne.

Hee would doe any office for the brethren if they (who hee knew had a strong purse, and his conscience waited on the strings of it, if all the zeale hee had) would beare him out in it: which they professed they would. Hee undertakes to ridd them of mine Host by one meanes or another. They gave him the best meanes they could, according to the present condition of the worke; and letters of credence to the favoures of that Sect in England; with which (his busines there being done, and his shipp cleared) hee hoyst the Sayles, and put to Sea: since which time mine Host has not troubled the brethren, but onely at the Counsell table: where now Sub indice lis est.

Chap. XXX.

Of Sir Christopher Gardiner Knight, and how hee spedd amongst the Seperatists.

SIr Christopher Gardiner, (a Knight, that had bin a traveller, both by Sea and Land; a good judicious gentleman in the Mathematticke, and other Sciences usefull for Plantations Kimistry, &c. and also being a practicall Enginer) came into those parts, intending discovery.

But the Seperatists love not those good parts when they proceede from a carnall man (as they call every good Protestant,) in shorte time had found the meanes to pick a quarrell with him. The meanes is, that they pursue to obtaine what they aime at: the word is there the meanes.

So that when they finde any man like to proove an enemy to their Church, and state, then straight the meanes must be used for defence. The first precept in their Politiques is, to defame the man at whom they aime, and then hee is a holy Israelite in their opinions, who can spread that fame brodest, like butter upon a loafe: no matter how thin; it will serve for a vaile: and then this man (who they have thus depraved) is a spotted uncleane leaper: hee must out, least hee pollute the Land, and them that are cleane.

If this be one of their guifts, then Machevill had as good gifts as they. Let them raise a scandall on any, though never so innocent; yet they know it is never wiped cleane out: the staind marks remaines: which hath bin well observed by one in these words of his:

Stick Candles gainst a Virgin walls white back:
If they'l not burne yet at the least they'l black.

And thus they dealt with Sir Christopher: and plotted by all the wayes, and meanes they could, to overthrow his undertakings in those parts.

And therefore I cannot chuse, but conclude, that these Seperatists have speciall gifts: for they are given to envy, and mallice extremely.

The knowledge of their defamacion could not please the gentleman well, when it came to his eare, which would cause him to make some reply, (as they supposed) to take exceptions at, as they did against Faire cloath: & this would be a meanes, they thought, to blow the coale, and so to kindle a brand that might fire him out of the Country too, and send him after mine Host of Ma-re-Mount.

They take occasion (some of them) to come to his howse when hee was gone up into the Country: and (finding hee was from home) so went to worke, that they left him neither howse nor habitation, nor servant, nor any thing to help him, if hee should retorne: but of that they had noe hope (as they gave it out) for hee was gone (as they affirmed) to leade a Salvage life; and for that cause tooke no company with him: and they, having considered of the matter, thought it not fit that any such man should live in so remoate a place, within the Compas of their patent. So they fired the place; and carried away the persons, and goods.

Sir Christopher was gone with a guide (a Salvage) into the inland parts for discovery: but, before hee was returned, hee met with a Salvage that told the guide, Sir Christopher would be killed: Master Temperwell (who had now found out matter against him) would have him dead or alive. This hee related; and would have the gentleman not to goe to the place appinted, because of the danger, that was supposed.

But Sir Christopher was nothing dismaid; hee would on, whatsoever come of it; and so met with the Salvages: and betweene them was a terrible skermish: But they had the worst of it, and hee scaped well enough.

The guide was glad of it, and learned of his fellowes that they were promised a great reward, for what they should doe in this imployment.

Which thing (when Sir Christopher understood,) hee gave thanks to God; and after (upon this occasion, to sollace himselfe) in his table booke, hee composed this sonnet, which I have here inserted for a memoriall.

THE SONNET.

WOlfes in Sheeps clothing why will ye,
Think to deceave God that doth see,
Your simulated sartity.
For my part I doe wish you could,
Your owne infirmities behold,
For then you would not be so bold,
Like Sophists why will you dispute,
With wisdome so, you doe confute,
None but yourselves: for shame be mute.
Least great Iehovah with his powre,
Do come upon you in a howre,
When you least think and you devoure.

This Sonnet the Gentleman composed, as a testimony of his love towards them, that were so ill affected towards him; from whome they might have receaved much good, if they had bin so wise to have imbraced him in a loving fashion.

But they despise the helpe, that shall come from a carnall man (as they termed him) who (after his retorne from those designes) finding how they had used him with such disrespect, tooke shipping, and disposed of himselfe for England, and discovered their practises in those parts towards his Majesties true harted Subjects, which they made wery of their aboade in those parts.

Chap. XXXI.

Of mine Host of Ma-re-Mount how hee played Ionas after hee had bin in the Whales belly for a time.

MIne Host of Ma-re-Mount being put to Sea; had delivered him, for his releafe by the way, (because the shipp was unvitteled, and the Seamen put to straight allowance, which could hold out, but to the Canaries) a part of his owne provision, being two moneths proportion; in all but 3. small peeces of porke, which made him expect to be famished before the voyage should be ended, by all likelyhood. Yet hee thought hee would make one good meale, before hee died: like the Colony servant in Virginea, that before hee should goe to the gallowes called to his wife to set on the loblolly pot, and let him have one good meale before hee went; who had committed a petty crime, that in those dayes, was made a cappitall offence.

And now mine Host being merrily disposed, on went the peeces of porke, where with hee feasted his body, and cherished the poore Sailers: and got out of them what Mr. Wethercock, their Master purposed to doe with him that hee had no more provision: & along they sailed from place to place, from Iland to Iland, in a pittifull wether beaten ship; where mine Host was in more dainger (without all question) then Ionas, when hee was in the Whales belly; and it was the great mercy of God that they had not all perished. Vittelled they were but for a moneth when they wayd Ancor, and left the first port.

They were a pray for the enemy for want of powther, if they had met them: besides the vessell was a very slugg, and so unserviceable, that the Master called a counsell of all the company in generall, to have theire opinions, which way to goe, and how to beare the helme, who all under their hand affirmed the shipp to be unserviceable: so that in fine the Master and men, and all were at their wits end about it: yet they imployed the Carpenters to search, and caulke her sides, and doe theire best whiles they were in her. Nine moneths they made a shife to use her, and shifted for supply of vittells at all the Islands they touched at; though it were so poorely, that all those helpes, and the short allowance of a bisket a day, and a few Lymons taken in at the Canaries, served but to bring the vessell in view of the lands end.

They were in such a desperat case, that (if God in his greate mercy had not favoured them, and disposed the windes faire untill the vessell was in Plimmouth roade,) they had without question perished; for when they let drop an Anchor, neere the Island of S. Michaels not one bit of foode left for all that starving allowance of this wretched wethercock, that if hee would have lanched out his beaver, might have bought more vittells in New England then he & the whole ship with the Cargazoun was worth, (as the passingers hee carried who vittelled themselves affirmed,) But hee played the miserable wretch, & had possessed his men with the contrary; who repented them of waying anchor before they knew so much.

Mine Host of Ma-re-Mount (after hee had bin in the Whales belly) was set a shore to see if hee would now play Ionas, so metamorphosed with a longe voyage, that hee looked like Lazarus in the painted cloath.

But mine Host (after due consideration of the premisses) thought it fitter for him to play Ionas in this kinde, then for the Seperatists to play Ionas in that kinde as they doe. Hee therefore bid Wethercock tell the Seperatists, that they would be made in due time to repent those malitious practises, and so would hee too; for hee was a Seperatist amongst the Seperatists as farre as his wit would give him leave; though when hee came in Company of basket makers, hee would doe his indevoure to make them pinne the basket, if hee could, as I have seene him. And now mine Host being merrily disposed, haveing past many perillous adventures in that desperat Whales belly, beganne in a posture like Ionas, and cryed Repent you cruell Seperatists repent, there are as yet but 40. dayes if Iove vouchsafe to thunder, Charter and the Kingdome of the Seperatists will fall asunder: Repent you cruell Schismaticks repent. And in that posture hee greeted them by letters retorned into new Canaan; and ever (as opportunity was fitted for the purpose) he was both heard & seene in the posture of Ionas against the crying repent you cruel Seperatists, repent, there are as yet but 40. dayes if Iove vouchsafe to thunder. The Charter and the Kingdome of the Seperatists will fall a sunder: Repent you cruell Schismaticks repent; If you will heare any more of this proclamation meete him at the next markettowne, for

Cynt hius aurem vellet.

A TABLE OF THE CONTENTS
OF THE THREE BOOKES.

The Tenents of the first Booke.

The Tenents of the second Booke.

The Tenents of the third Booke.

F I N I S .

CPSIA information can be obtained
at www.ICGtesting.com
Printed in the USA
JSHW041119050521
14349JS00002B/101

9 781429 045667